AWESOME WOMEN ON THE MOVE

# NATIONAL
# PRAYER BOOK

PRAYING FOR

*Everything under the Sun*

## TENARIA DRUMMOND-SMITH
Prayers from 52 Women

HOV
PUBLISHING

HOV Publishing a division of HOV, LLC.
www.hovpub.com / hopeofvision@gmail.com

Cover Design: Chantelle Roberts for Xcelled Designs
Editor/Proofreader: Jeff Smith and HOV Publishing

Contact the author Tenaria Drummond-Smith at:
tds@awesomewomenonthemove.org and FB: @AwesomeWomenOnTheMove

For more information about special discounts for bulk purchases,
please contact Tenaria Drummond-Smith or hopeofvision@gmail.com

Paperback ISBN: 978-1-942871-78-1
eBook ISBN: 978-1-942871-79-8

Library of Congress Control Number:

10    9    8    7    6    5    4    3    2

Printed in the United States of America

# Endorsement

Grace and peace from our Lord Jesus Christ.

Sister Tenaria Smith, I want to congratulate you on your new Awesome Women On The Move Prayer Book release. I believe that your hand is on the right pulse of the time that we are living in.

Prayer allows us direct access to God and this is what we need, a direct entrance to God. When we pray, we are basically having a conversation with God. There is no right or wrong way to pray, nor are there any universal phrases to use or special requirements to follow. Prayer is a privilege given by God that allows us to build a relationship with Him.

So, let us move into our prayer positions and read the prayers downloaded into the hearts of these precious women of God. May every word be lifted into the heavens, let souls be strengthened and people be made whole. God bless you daughter, may you continue to seek after the will of God.

Bishop Derrick Farmer, DD
Senior Pastor, Christ Pentecostal Temple

# Endorsement

Greetings in the matchless name of Jesus! To all who have the pleasure of reading the words from the pages of this book, I pray that God breathes a fresh wind of the Spirit into your lives. I prophetically speak that what you read in this book meets you wherever you are because the power of God supersedes time and space. So, in whatever year, season, or place you may encounter this God-inspired book, my prayer is that God meets your need. As this book goes out to the nations, we pray that you be a part of this awesome move. I encourage you to soak up what this prayer book has to offer you spiritually.

I pray that the Father opens your ears in the realm of the Spirit so you can hear his voice clearly. I pray that the Father help you hear whatever instructions he has for you and for whatever corrections you might need to make in your life. Open up your eyes in the Spirit so you can see what he wants you to see. I pray that as you read this text, God will show you a glimpse of your destiny.

My prayer for you is that the Father help you to be sensitive to the smell of his presence and to let your prayer time be a sweet-smelling fragrance unto him. Let this prophetic text awaken and sharpen your discernment. Let this prayer book awaken the gifts he has placed in you. Finally, be prayerful as God downloads instructions from heaven on how this book should be used in your life!

May God bless you and heaven smile on you in Jesus' name!

Stephen Quinones, B.S., M.S. Ed
Minister, Christ Pentecostal Temple

# Foreword

I am humbled to present this book to you. You are reading a collection of prayers from Awesome Women On The Move presents... "National Prayer Book: Praying for Everything Under The Sun". As we celebrate Women's History Month, allow these women to share prayers that will heal, deliver, and set you free. Everything that is happening in our nation, in the world, and I am sure in your life, is covered by prayer in this book. If you open your heart, these prayers will resonate with you and change your life.

I have known Prophetess Tenaria Drummond-Smith since she was a young girl. She was always energetic and attentive to her grandmother. Today, she stands strong on the shoulders of great praying women. Open your heart to receive these prayers that will catapult you into the presence of Almighty God and bless you when you come out of your prayer chamber. Tenaria, God bless you, and may God continue to use you as you fulfill your purpose in helping women to reach their destiny in God.

Apostle Dr. Patricia A. Wiley
Senior Pastor/Organizer, Oil of Joy Ministries II, Inc.
Presiding Prelate, Oil of Joy Ministries II International Alliance

# Preface

So here we are again with another project that Tenaria has birthed and nurtured. Time has passed us by, but it has been time made useful in the construction and fruition of one project after the other as our God gives her visions. It has been—and continues to be—my role to stand in witness and support of everything that Tenaria moves forth in, even when some things may not be so clear to me in the beginning.

To date, this book has been our most intensive and large-scale undertaking yet. This is a great accomplishment for us, for our publisher Germaine Miller-Summers of Hope of Vision Publishing, and for every participating co-author who sacrificed and labored in prayer to speak life into this project's bones. This book manifests as proof of what was decreed in Tenaria's first book, "I've Been Hurt In The Church". As husband and friend, I know more than anyone else could know: God is not done being glorified through this daughter. No, not yet.

The LORD saith in Jeremiah 29:12 (KJV), "Then shall ye call upon me, and ye shall go and pray unto me, and I will hearken unto you.", and we invite you to know for yourself that what God has spoken is true. Prayer works! For those who already know, we invite you to go deeper in prayer to ascend higher. I pray that this collective, prophetic effort blesses, encourages and strengthens readers' hearts and minds in the knowledge, presence, peace, and power of our Lord Jesus Christ. To God alone be all glory, power, praise and dominion. May the grace and peace of our God rest upon every reader of this book. Amen.

Jeff Smith
Co-founder of Awesome Women On The Move

# Content

Note: *As the co-authors, most of whom are unfamiliar to one another, prayed according to the heart of God, signs of the times are demonstrated in the  coincidence of some recurring themes.*

# ABOUT THE AWESOME WOMEN ON THE MOVE
# National Prayer Book

Tenaria Drummond-Smith, founder and visionary of Awesome Women On The Move: God give me the vision to do this Awesome Women On The Move Prayer Book with fifty women because prayer is my life and it is what I do. I love the fact that I can speak directly to God and how He speaks back to me, and having said that, I know I am not alone. God told me that it is imperative that the book covers everything that I can imagine and think of. Everyone that God has allowed to participate in this prayer book was assigned to pray for certain issues that His people deal with. Someone must stand in the gap for something that we might have seen, or heard, or experienced.

The Bible is clear about there being nothing new under the sun. What we are experiencing in our lives is prophecy being fulfilled. I still believe in the power of prayer, even when it looks like God has stopped moving.  It is my desire for everyone who reads this prophetic Awesome Women On The Move Prayer Book to feel the power of anointed prayer coming from these pages. I pray that this book will reach the four corners of the earth. I pray that every prayer will be answered and people's lives will be changed. God will use the answered prayers as testimonies that God still answers prayers. People will know that prayer still works.

Lord, I ask you bless this project so that THIS PRAYER BOOK SHALL BE WRITTEN IN DIFFERENT LANGUAGES. Amen, and amen."For where two or three are gathered together in my name, there am I in the midst of them of them." (Matthew 18:20 KJV)

# Authors

PRAYER BY: TENARIA DRUMMOND-SMITH

Yes Lord, I thank you right now in the mighty name of Jesus. You said that we can do all things through you, and that we shall be the head and not the tail in the mighty name of Jesus. Lord, I ask that you give those who have a story to tell the faith to step out and write their first book in the name of Jesus. Lord, let them not be afraid, please help them to put their thoughts on paper. O God, you haven't given us a spirit of fear, but of love, and power, and a sound mind. O God, I ask you to stir up those who read this prayer to begin to write immediately because their story could help another person who might be going through a similar situation.

O God, you tell us in your word to write the vision and make it plain, glory be to God. Lord, help every author's story go forth to do your will and all for your glory. I pray in the name of Jesus that their books reach the four corners of the earth. The books shall be written in every language in the mighty name of Jesus. O God, let their books be turned into plays and movies. Lord, we know that that there is nothing impossible for you to do. I declare that someone's story will receive Emmy Awards for a movie or short film. You can do it Lord, because you own the heaven and the earth. Lord, you said we have not because we ask not, so I'm asking for everything in faith in Jesus' mighty name, amen.

Scriptural references: Psalm 84:11; Habakkuk 2:2

# Homeless

PRAYER BY: SOPHIA L. GREENE

Praise be to the One who giveth and taketh. Lord, as I sit in your presence with humility, I look to you for all answers that I seek. I thank you for my home and the coverage you have prepared for me. Father God, I bring to you all souls who are without a home or in between homes. Father, we ask that you give them the strength to push through the day and rely on your promises. You said you will be our rock and anchor in our times of need, and we believe you. You said you would never leave us nor forsake us, and we believe you. You are the promise keeper and not a liar. Today, we place all people who have lost their homes before you in prayer. They depend solely on you for provision. Father, walk though all corners of the world and comfort all who feel hopeless in this time of their lives.

No matter where we are in our walk with you, there is hope in God every day. Never let us forget that a house or a life without you is a life of homelessness. Living with you in our lives and acknowledging you every day while striving to obey your word is the true feeling of having a home. Father we thank you and we adore you. You are exceedingly worthy to be praised. In your arms is the true home and with you, our cups are filled and running over each day. Shalom.

# Clarity

PRAYER BY: ROBERTA JONES-JOHNSON

Hallelujah! Father God in the name of Jesus, I come to you praising your holy name and thanking you for giving me life today. I ask for your forgiveness where I fall short. Continue to pour into me so I'll be more like you and less like myself. You're the great God above all, the only One deserving all the honor and praise.

Father, I come to you asking for clarity and focus in the life of your people. The world places so many distractions in front of us that cause us to lose focus. Father, I ask that your Holy Spirit allows us to push those distractions and people aside and enable us to focus on what's important in our lives and focus on you. Father, I rebuke every noise, every circumstance, and every spirit that tries to block our concentration. I pray for our strength in ridding our surroundings of people who don't want us to be joined to you and to succeed.

Father, I pray that your will be done in our lives. We forever give you the glory. Help us maintain our vision and focus on doing all that you expect us to do. I pray that we take control over our wandering thoughts. Guide us in our words, our thoughts, and our actions. Father, help us prioritize our life situations, issues, and circumstances. According to your will, help us separate our needs from our wants. Help us focus on your voice as you give us direction for our lives.

Father God, you're the God of order who helps us keep our lives in order. Help us organize the home and the workplace. Help us remove confusion and interruptions. Help us walk away from distractions caused by spirits. Lord, you tell us that no weapon formed against us shall prosper, and we stand on your word. I pray that we meditate on your word and see clearly enough not to take on more things than we can handle. We're new creatures in Christ, and our former ways are no more. Lord, help us to be a blessing to others. Help us surround ourselves with people who share our visions. We praise you because our success comes through you. I pray all these things and give thanks in Jesus' name. Amen.

Scriptural reference: Isaiah 54:17

# Generation Curses

PRAYER BY: PROPHETESS VON BRAND

Father, we thank you today for being our covering, and for being our hedge of protection as we stand together in unity to break the back of Satan. You said that where two or three gather in your name, we can be assured that you are in the midst, so we want to acknowledge your very presence. Lord, you told us that we can come boldly to the throne of grace with confidence so that we may receive mercy and find grace to help us in our time of need. We need you on today Jesus, as we come against generational curses.

You let us know of a truth, that whatsoever we bind on earth will be bound in heaven and whatsoever we loose on earth will be loosed in heaven. Therefore we bind those spirits of bitterness, rebellion, strife, control, rejection, accusation, jealousy, depression, poverty, worry, doubt, mental illness, paranoia, gluttony, cults, sexual impurity, covetousness, nervousness, persecution, false religion, cursing, infirmity, death, inheritance by physical, emotional, or mental abuse, competition, and every other generational curse. We command for them to leave now in the mighty name of Jesus! Father, we loose your people from everything that their forefathers did that came through the bloodline. It stops with them and it stops today! Neither will their children nor their children's children have to be subjected to that strongman. We know that Satan comes to kill, steal, and destroy, but you came so that we may have life and have it more abundantly.

Lord, we thank you because we know that you can do anything

but fail. We thank you for being a miracle worker and for lifting our heads. We thank you for setting us free from the bondage of our past. You said that if the Son sets us free, we will be free indeed. We thank you for knowing that whatever we ask for in prayer, if we believe that we have received it, it will be ours. Lord, we believe. Father, as we seal this prayer in the blood of Jesus, we thank you for allowing us to come into your presence. In Jesus' name we pray, amen.

# Youth

PRAYER BY: ANNETTA DRUMMOND

Father, we praise you, we worship you, and we bless your holy name. Father, we stand in the gap for our youth. You called the young because they are strong. I ask you in confidence to keep them strong and alert in everything they say and do. May they be able to persevere through their teenage years and trust you to keep them able to withstand the lies and traps of the enemy in Jesus' name.

Father, I pray you will keep our youth's minds stayed on you. Help them flee sexual immorality and keep themselves pure to reserve the gift of sex for marriage. You are able to keep them from falling and present them faultless before your throne in glory. Let it be it done for them in Jesus' name.

Father, I pray you will uphold our youth in your likeness and in your image. Let them be more like you in the earth realm. Use them as arrows in your bow in the spirit realm. Use them for your honour and glory, and set them apart to go forth and win souls in your name. Lead back the ones who have gone astray from you. Father, wash with your unconditional love. Dispatch your angels to watch over them and keep them in all their ways. I ask you touch, heal and deliver those who have troubled minds and are struggling with their mental health, drug abuse, promiscuity, pornography, and abandonment. Let your Holy Spirit heal them at the root of their troubles. Touch their minds. Set them free to worship you in the beauty of holiness as you have created them. Guide them in all their endeavours in Jesus' name.

For those who are incarcerated, remind them of your grace and mercy. Let them know that you are their hope. Send your angels to comfort them and keep their minds stayed on you. I pray that they will know that Jesus Lord and Savior, and commit their lives to your authority. Teach them to how to have an intimate relationship with you. Father, rebuild what is broken in them in Jesus' name. Amen.

# Human Rights

PRAYER BY: QUEEN MOTHER

We call on you, the Divine force within us, to be a just people. Help us to be righteous and just towards each other. God, hear our prayers and grant our supplications. We come as children seeking your mercy and your divine intervention. Hear our prayer of love and fairness towards one another. We know that you are a just God, a God of mercy and love. O God, forgive us all of our sins and transgressions against you and against one another. Let us be like you, reflect the image of yourself in us to be just towards one another. Show us how to show humility by caring for each other with love and respect. We may have different religions, cultures and traditions, but teach us how to love each other. We seek your just ways.

Creator, we all have a right to have food. We have a right to be clothed and sheltered from the elements of life. O Lord, you knew us before we were ever known and conceived in our mothers' wombs. We pray to you to keep us on the sacred path with a sound and just mind. Deliver us from causing harm and danger to one another. Help us to cultivate a love toward one another that is just and fair. Be merciful to us as we gain a better understanding of life. Help us to have a divine consciousness of human rights. What we want for ourselves, we should want for others. God, let us be your justice to speak of your justice and fairness. Amen.

# Imprisonment

PRAYER BY: JANET LENNOX

Abba Father, we thank you and praise you for who you are, the God of the Universe, and the Father of Abraham, Isaac and Jacob. We come to you in no other name but the name of Jesus Christ of Nazareth. We ask you to forgive us from known, hidden, and presumptuous sins in the name of Jesus. Father, we come against the spirit of imprisonment, whether it attacks us physically, spiritually, mentally, or financially. We subdue the powers of darkness that imprison us with the blood of Jesus. Lord God, when Paul and Silas worshipped you while they were imprisoned, you opened up the gates of the prison. Lord God, we worship you and command those doors that close us in to be opened right now in Jesus' name.

Spirit of imprisonment that causes restriction, depravity and suffering, we nullify and denounce you for closing doors that keep us from our destined place of progress. Spirits of restriction, depravity, suffering and destruction, loose your hold right now in Jesus' name. Holy Spirit, have your way in our lives. We walk out of every prison situation right now in the name of Jesus. By the blood of Jesus, we command wicked forces that contend with us to overcome us to be scattered by the fire of God right now. We call upon the blood of Jesus to be poured out in every part of our lives where Satan has imprisoned us. We now walk in our freedom because whosoever God sets free is free indeed. Thank you, Jesus, for your loving kindness and tender mercies that keep us always in Jesus' name. Amen.

# Elders

PRAYER BY: DAWN GRANTHAM

Father God in the precious name of Jesus, protect our elders. If they have to go out without any supervision, even if it's just to the grocery store, protect them O Lord! Let no one have the chance to take their belongings or hurt them like we see on the news. Let none of these men be so cruel and try to rape our elderly women. They need help Lord, please help them. Stop them in their tracks the next time they try to do harm. Distract them so that they forget what their intentions were. O Lord, reach down and touch people's hearts to give up their seats on the trains and buses for our elderly. They should not have to stand holding on for dear life while healthy young people sit around them.

O Lord, have mercy for our elderly because you know all about them. Let your angels descend from heaven and encamp around them as they go to and fro. Keep them out of harm's way. If our elderly need help crossing the street, send the right people in their path who are willing and happy to help them from the heart. Touch the hearts and minds of loved ones to see elderly family members who might be in hospitals and nursing homes, feeling alone and as if nobody cares about them. O Lord, have mercy on them. For those who have home attendant care, give them the best care ever. Bless their home attendants with patience and knowledge. Bless them with the understanding of how to treat their patients' needs and value their lives as if they were their own family and friends. O Lord, please remember the elderly who are locked up in prison and the ones who are homeless. Send your people to minister to them and help them get their lives together. O Lord, I ask all these things in the precious name of Jesus. Amen!

Scriptural reference: Psalm 121

# Victims

PRAYER BY: MIRANDA RIVERS

Lord, we pray for those who lost their lives from natural disasters. We pray for those who lost their lives to senseless violence. We pray for victims who survived and are traumatized. We live in these times where random killings, shootings, and terrorist attacks are the norm. Father God, we come to you as humbly as we know how. We ask that you touch the hearts of those whose lives have been devastated. We keep in our hearts our loved ones whose lives has been changed because of the loss of their loved ones. We ask you to wrap your arms around these families and comfort them. Help transform their minds and hearts so that they can feel your presence. Lord, remove the heaviness from their hearts. Bless those who have survived and are striving to have the courage to face the days ahead. Bless those victims that have continued to live in spite of their devastation.

Every day we leave our homes and return safely is a blessing, so God, we give you thanks. It's hard not to live in fear when we see senseless acts of violence all around us. We see people killing people because of hatred and terrorism against society. Father God, you're the giver of life and peace. We ask you to soften the hearts and steady the minds of those who commit violence of hate against your people. Replace the hate in their hearts with love, replace their violence with peace, replace their darkness with light. Help them to know your presence and help them to become children of God. We ask all these things in Jesus' name. Amen.

Scriptural references: Psalm 23:4, 34:14, 140:1,4

# Forgiveness

PRAYER BY: SARAH NICHOLS

Our Father, we enter into your gates with thanksgiving and into your courts with praise. You're so awesome, you're so great, and we praise your holy name. Thank you for your faithfulness. You're the Alpha and the Omega, the beginning and the end. The Author and finisher of our faith, the originator of our beginning and end. You're so worthy of all praise and glory. Father, we love and thank you for who you are. We ask you for the forgiveness of our sins and our cleansing from all unrighteousness. We thank you for your son Jesus for showing us the greatest gifts of forgiveness in your word. We thank you for the gift of your Holy Spirit that helps, comforts, teaches and leads us unto all truth.

Thank you for your gift of forgiveness by giving us the gift of your Son Jesus Christ, who gave his life for us so that we might be forgiven. Father, thank you for the grace and mercy that you give us each day. As you have loved and forgiven us unconditionally, help us to be able to forgive those who hurt us. Father, help us to release the hurt and begin to love as Jesus loves. Help us to deal with our emotions so they might not control our actions. Lord, teach us how to let the peace that comes from Christ rule in our hearts. When we forgive with our words, allow your Holy Spirit to fill our hearts with peace. God, as we draw closer to you, help us to let go of unforgiveness. With gratitude, let us see the good in people and find compassion that comes with true forgiveness. Help us to be mindful of this prayer when we see the people who hurt us so we can have your thoughts toward them. We thank you for healing us right now and perfecting our love in forgiveness. We thank you for healing our bodies of sickness or disease due to unforgiveness. We thank you because stress will no longer be part of our lives, and how the peace of God that passes all understanding will replace it. We give you honor and praise. We love you Lord, and we're grateful. In Jesus' name, amen.

# Dysfunctional Families

PRAYER BY: CAMEO BOONE

Father, I come to you in prayer in the precious name of Jesus, thanking you for breath and life. I thank you for the opportunity to come to you on behalf of the dysfunctional family. Elohim, as a Black woman, I understand how slavery has taken a large portion of our identity and created our lack and dysfunction in society. I realize that it was not by chance that slavery was used to oppress, control, and divide the family, and made the black man vulnerable. Father, I also understand that a lot of our people have turned their backs on you since the beginning. We have allowed society to shape our thoughts and lives. Satan has set up a world system that denounces you in school and in the home. I pray that families will pray more and read your word together. In Jesus' name, I come up against any satanic views through media that are influencing the family! I come against the exploitation of our talents in Jesus' name! Thank you for our gifts and talents that will glorify you! Father, give us the desire to serve you so we can eliminate family dysfunction!

Thank you, Jesus, for strengthening the family in this satanic system that makes it hard for us to provide and survive. I rebuke poverty and living check- to-check in Jesus' name! I rebuke divorce and domestic violence in our families. I rebuke drugs and alcohol abuse in front of our children. Father, you would never build a system for us to toil in or compromise our morals and beliefs in order to obtain riches. This system was not built for us! I thank you because we won't have to compromise any longer, Jesus! I pray for the covering of the blood of Jesus over our families! I thank you God, because you knew these things would happen before the foundation of the world! Thank you for giving the family a way out! Thank you giving us a plan to build communities that serve you and run self-sufficiently from this system, like the Hebrews had in the land of Goshen. I thank you because we have victory over this system, knowing that you will never leave or forsake us. Thank you for the deliverance of the dysfunctional family, Elohim. Amen.

Scriptural references: Genesis 45:3-10, 47:6; Deuteronomy 31:6

# Backsliders

PRAYER BY: CYRINTHIA HILL-FLOWERS

Lord Jesus, restore the backslider that has left their first love. Bring them back to you, the one that will keep them, deliver them, and set them free. Restore their prayer life and their walk in you. JESUS, Forgive them for letting go! Forgive them for no longer trusting in you. Jesus, the circumstance that caused them to turn back, I'm asking you to remove it far from them. I come in Jesus' name armed with the sword of the Spirit and the word of God, knowing that you are married to the backslider. Help the backslider to seek your face dear God, call them back to you. Fill them with your power, and your anointing. Jesus, give them the strength to stand and make that step back to you.

God, we come against everything and every spirit that will cause your people to turn back. We bind discouragement, disappointment, anger, unforgiveness, hopelessness, mistrust, and hurt in the church that made souls leave the body of Christ because of it. Father in the name of Jesus, we declare healing, and by faith, we believe that those that have turned back are coming back to you. Jesus, we reclaim souls for the kingdom. Everyone that has experienced hurt in these areas is healed in Jesus' name. Father, they are letting go of the pain, and you are penetrating their hearts and blessing each and every soul. I pray that they will receive clear instructions to give their life back to you in Jesus' name. Lord, let them experience your grace and mercy. Don't let them miss out on your promise, plan and purpose for their lives.

Father, help them know that you still love them with an everlasting love. All the plans that the enemy has used to pull your people out of relationship is broken now in Jesus' name and it will no longer prosper. Thank you, Jesus, that heaven is rejoicing over every soul that comes back to you. Thank you for removing the pain, and the shame, and replacing it with your peace, love, joy, happiness, and forgiveness. Most of all, that they will feel the love of Christ once again, now and forever more in in the mighty name of Jesus. Amen!

Scriptural references: Jeremiah 3:14, 29:11; Galatians 5:22-23, 6:1; Luke 18:1; Proverbs 3:5-6; Hebrews 4:12; Ephesians 6:17-18; 2 Kings 4:12; Matthew 15:24; Psalm 32:8; 2 Corinthians 12:9

# Headaches

PRAYER BY: JOYCE ROLLINS

God, thank you for your mercy and your grace. Thank you for a new opportunity to come before your throne. Lord you are holy, you are righteous. I give you glory, honor and praise for you alone are worthy. You are matchless, and you are merciful. You are loving, and you are kind. You are the only way and the truth. You are the life. God, there's no healing without you. Thank you for never for leaving us. Thank you for hearing our petitions and for sending us answers. I call upon you as the Great Physician, the God who heals every disease. I come to you concerning headaches. I know that sickness is not of you. I know that you're a healer. Despite sickness and pain, you are God. I speak to you, spirit of headache, and command you to flee. I curse you and your assignment back to the pit of hell. I speak directly to the imp attached to the nerve; release yourself in the name of Jesus. I take authority over every demon that causes inflammation. I speak to every blockage and closed passageway, to every obstruction; I command you to open up in the name of Jesus. I speak to the enemy; I declare your assignment null and void in the name of the Lord Jesus.

God, I speak healing over the lives of your people. Every underlying ailment that causes headaches, I command you to lose your hold. Lord, pour out the balm of Gilead and send healing. God, I cry out to you on behalf of those suffering from sinus headaches, stress headaches, migraines, high pressure headaches; be healed in the name of the Lord Jesus.

Your word says you'll heal us and save us because we praise you. I open my mouth in praise to you Abba! asking you to accept my praise on behalf of those who need healing from headaches. We thank you for restoration. God, we thank you in advance because your goodness never fails. Thank you for divine healing from headaches. Thank you for making us whole. AND IT IS SO IN JESUS' NAME. AMEN!

Scriptural references: Jeremiah 17:14, 30:17

# Favor

PRAYER: CHERYLN OLIVER-McKAY

Heavenly Father, as we come boldly come to the throne of grace, first and foremost, we want to thank you for life, health and strength. We want to thank you for waking us up this morning, and we're praying for favor on today! Lord God, this world needs your favor. There are so many people who are going through tough situations right now. Oh God, there are so many things that the devil is trying to do us here on Earth. Lord God, we ask that you rebuke the devil right now in Jesus' name. Heavenly Father, you said in your word that whosoever finds you will find his life and shall obtain favor in the Lord. We're asking for your favor. You also said in your word that good understanding giveth favor, but the way of the transgressor is hard. Lord God, we don't need our lives to be any harder than it already is. We're calling on you right now in the name of Jesus to remove the burdens from us.

You said in your word that a good man shows favor and lendeth, and he will guide his affairs with discretion. Lord God, for each and every one praying in secret, you know their hearts and they know that you're the only one who can do anything in their lives. Many people are seeking after people when they should be seeking after you. I come right now praying that they would open up their hearts and minds to you Lord God, for it is only with you that they'll be able to know the peace that will surpass understanding, the favor, and the wisdom that only you can give them. I pray all these things in Jesus' name. Amen.

Scriptural references: Psalm 112:5; Proverbs 8:35; Philippians 4:7

# Pandemics

PRAYER BY: ESTHER BURGESS

Heavenly Father, we give you thanks for another day, knowing that with each day, there are new mercies we see. Because tomorrow is not promised to anyone, we give you glory, honor and thanks to you who live forever and ever. We thank you for the breath we breathe, the air, the wind that blows and the exchange that takes place to filter the air. Lord, there are so many things happening in the earth. There are many diseases we never heard of that are on the rise, and mankind is fast losing grip on life as we know it. There are also sicknesses, poverty, pestilence, devastation, blood in our streets. We have this new coronavirus pandemic that the world is experiencing. Because of this virus, there is an intrusion to the essence of our breath. We don't really know much about it except the name given. It's not restricted, and has affected nations, both rich and poor, young and old, and even transcends cultures.

Lord, have mercy upon us and save us, for you are our help and source of our survival. Lord, I plead the blood of Jesus against this coronavirus and everything that comes with it. I pray that every contrary wind that drives it is abated. Blood-wash the atmosphere and filter the air, make it conducive to life so that we can breathe. I pray that as we breathe, our respiratory system is filtered and free from any particles of this virus. I pray that our noses, throats, and sinuses will be free from every foreign particle seen and unseen that comes to invade and disrupt. O Lord have mercy upon us, watch over us and protect us from this invasion in Jesus' name. I know that nothing is impossible for you, so we stand on your word, that though we will walk through the valley of the shadow of death, we will fear no evil, because thou art with us, thy rod and thy staff they comfort us. O Lord I pray that people will turn unto to you from this pandemic, that you might heal our land. I pray that they will know that you are the only true and living God, and that you have breathed into us the breath of life. O Lord hear, O Lord heal, O Lord save in Jesus' mighty and matchless name. Amen.

Scriptural reference: Psalm 23:4

# Suicide

PRAYER BY: THERESA BYRD

Our Father who art in heaven, I'm calling on your holy name with my head bowed down, my eyes closed, and with a crying heart. So many of your children nowadays are attempting suicide as their way out. When I hear the word, it sends chills up and down my spine. It's a scary situation to even think about. LORD, please touch their minds and hearts today. Cover them with your blood in their going out, their coming in, in their laying down as well as their rising up.

This is a vicious cycle taking place all around the world. LORD, I know that you're the only one who can stop this madness. All of them have different reasons, but the load must be too heavy for any of them to bear. You are an awesome God who knows all things. I'm praying for them and hoping that you send the Comforter their way. They're in need of being saved. LORD, strengthen them; show them the way. Please lift them up for your glory. Amen.

Scriptural reference: Psalm 61:1-2

# Soul Ties

PRAYER BY: PASTOR SHAWN QUALLO

Father in the mighty name of Jesus, I come thanking you for your mercy and your Grace. I bless your Holy name; Lord you are high and lifted up. We exalt you above every name, and we exalt you above every situation. You are the burden-bearer and the heavy load lifter! I come now rebuking and loosing your people from every ungodly soul tie. Whatsoever we bind on earth is bound in heaven, and whatsoever we loose on earth is loosed in heaven. Right now, we bind now every soul tie, and every relationship that was made known or unknown through demonic activities. We cancel the works of darkness that keep your people bound to every wicked spirit covenant.   We destroy the works of darkness and demonic soul ties. Our struggle is not against flesh and blood, but against the rulers, against the authorities, against the powers of this dark world and against the spiritual forces of evil in the heavenly realms. We cancel the works of demonic soul ties in Jesus' name. We call forth the fire of God to destroy every wicked stronghold at the root in Jesus' name.

Lord, every relationship of the past that was not ordained by you, we destroy their memory right now and we deactivate its power! The blood of Jesus washes over our minds, our hearts, our wills and emotions. Lord, your name is a strong tower for the righteous to run in and be kept safe. We loose and destroy the chains that bind your people to keep them from their divine purpose and covenant relationships ordained by God. No more delays or setbacks. We call Kingdom marriages to come forth to be one flesh, and not one soul. Purify hearts and minds now, Lord. Cause your word to be a lamp for our feet, and a light to our path that will expose every trap the enemy has set before your people. Every wicked soul tie reaching back through ten generations, we destroy those contracts by fire in Jesus' name. Lord, open our eyes and give us 20/20 vision in the spirit realm to see the tricks of the enemy going forward. We thank you because hearts are healed now in Jesus' mighty name. Amen.

Scriptural references: Matthew 18:18; Ephesians 6:12; Genesis 2:24

# Grandchildren

PRAYER BY: JACQUELENE SCRUGGS

Lord, we come before you, thanking and praising you for waking us up each and every morning. We thank you for keeping us all through the night. You didn't have to do it, but we thank you for doing it. Lord, we thank you for being so good to us. We come to you with thanksgiving in our hearts. Thank you for making a way out of no way. Thank you, Father, for giving us grandchildren who are a joy to have. We thank you for keeping them from all hurt, harm, and danger seen and unseen. Thank you, Jesus, glory hallelujah. Keep our grandchildren safe as they travel to and from school, and everywhere they go. Lord, we thank you for everything you have done for them. Shape our grandchildren with love. We pray that you keep your arms of protection around them.

Lord, we need to teach our grandchildren the right way to go because if we don't, the world will show them every wrong way. There is so much wickedness in the world today. Jesus, touch our grandchildren with the finger of God. They are faced with life challenges every day. They are faced with peer pressure, bullying, and being discriminated against. We need to keep our grandchildren lifted up in prayer before you. We can't stop praying for them as well as we pray for one another. Lord, you are our way-maker. Thank you for guiding us. Thank you for never leaving us or forsaking us, and for being with us always. You are in control. Lord, we thank you, glory hallelujah. Jesus, you are our life and our salvation. Grandchildren are a blessing, and we thank you for what you have given us. Lord, we trust you for their needs because nothing is impossible for you. We ask you for all these blessings in the name of Jesus. Amen.

Scriptural references: Matthew 19:14; Proverbs 17:6

# Resentment

PRAYER BY: WENDYANN WILLIAMS

Dear Lord Jesus, our hearts ache from the injustice brought before us. Our hearts grow weary. Our thoughts consume us. The anger and resentment we feel about our offenders won't go away as fast as we want it to. It feels like a wave of the ocean's undertow, pulling us under, deeper and faster into this cruel depth of bitterness. The pain from the hurt runs deep, suffocating us and poisoning our very being. How long do we have to go through what feels like an agony of defeat? How long must we carry this sorrow in our hearts and wrestle with our thoughts? How long will our adversaries continue to have power over us? How long will the enemy's evil deeds and words continue to have power over our minds? Sometimes we feel depleted and alone in this situation, and the pain just won't go away.

Resentment has stirred up within and a righteous indignation along with it. This righteous anger morphs into a rigor mortis, paralyzing us. Our hearts secretly want revenge, and a war wages within. And though we know harboring a grudge may feel good, there is no reward from it because the hurt still lies beneath surface. Therefore, Lord, as my Helper, I beg you to guide us and change us despite this rotten situation. Help us get rid of this anger and resentment. Help us put a training leash on it. Guide us by the power of your Holy Spirit and change us. Help us trust in your unfailing love to get through this. Encourage us with your word of wisdom and show us how to deal with this situation. Show us how to remain obedient to your calling. Please comfort us while we patiently wait on you for healing. Fill our hearts with thanksgiving so that we may have the faith in your peace that never fails.

Thank you for hearing my prayer, for being a concerned God, a loving Father in whom we can trust. I know there is nothing to hard or impossible for you to do because you are our healer, our helper, and our restorer of broken pieces. There's nothing impossible for you to do. I'm so grateful that you understand our deepest woes and cares about every area of this life. I praise you, and I lift you up. Amen.

# Joy

PRAYER BY: SHERRELL D. MIMS

Heavenly Father, as we enter this prayer, we ask you to forgive us of any unforgiveness, bitterness, malice, sin, and bad attitude in our hearts so that our prayers may be heard and answered. Heavenly Father, from the north, south, east and west, we come together in prayer. From every region of the earth, we come together touching and agreeing to bring your word back to remembrance. O LORD, we thank you because your word does not return to you void and that it shall accomplish that which you please.

Heavenly Father, we thank you for the joy you give us; that unspeakable joy in our hearts that no man can take away. We are reminded of our joy through the Word whom we have not seen, but love. In your glory, we rejoice with joy unspeakable. Jesus, you are the reason for the smile on our faces, the laughter in our hearts, and the joy and happiness that we can continue to have throughout the day or night. If we had ten-thousand tongues, we still could not thank you enough. LORD, you went to the cross for all of us so we could have love, joy, peace and happiness. No one but you could have done this. LORD, because of your perfect sacrifice for the world, we declare that we will show the fruit of the Spirit. Now LORD, we seal this prayer in the almighty, majestic, and magnificent name of Jesus Christ, knowing our prayers have been answered. Hallelujah! Amen, and so be it!

Scriptural references: Romans 15:13; Isaiah 55:11; Matthew 18:20; Psalm 118:24; I Peter 1:8; Galatians 5:22-23

# Wisdom

PRAYER BY: D.D. HOUSTON DUPREE

Heavenly Father, I come to you today with an open heart and mind to pray for your people to acquire as much wisdom as they can. The more wisdom we acquire, the more our spirits will be open to receive your blessings. I thank you, dear Father, for the friends and family members who have been with us throughout our formative years and have given us the knowledge of their experiences for our advantage. Please send people into our lives who will encourage and motivate us to seek those blessings you have waiting for us.

I pray that the wisdom we possess, and look forward to receiving, will be imparted to others we encounter so they could use it for their own advancement. When we don't know the answer to certain life issues, I pray that your Spirit will lead us to the Bible for answers. I know we don't have the answers to our questions all the time, but when we speak to you, you uplift our spirits. You encourage us to accept those unanswered questions while we wait for the answer from heaven in your time. Amen.

# Bullying
PRAYER BY: JEAN THOMPSON

My faithful Father, I love singing praises to you. I give thanks for your love, peace, joy, and happiness. I know that your favor and grace endure forever. Lord, I'll always praise you because you made all of us fearfully and wonderfully. As I kneel in prayer for the world, I have such exhilaration in my heart to know the unfailing grace that you give us. My heart, mind, and soul rest all day on the daily provisions you provide not only for me and my loved ones, but for the entire world.

the pain of bully victims. God, in your mighty power, remove all aspects of bullying from the church, the workplace, schools, and in our homes. Father, we need your guidance and protection at all times of the day and night Jesus, there's so much pain in the world. I'm standing in the gap for those who are being bullied, and for those who do the bullying. I ask in your merciful name as our Creator to help us now and ease, even as we sleep. We thank you because we can depend on your promised word to love us and protect us. We know that you'll never leave or forsake us. Amen.

Scriptural references: Psalm 139:14; Mark 12:30-31; Luke 6:27-31

# Strength of Women

PRAYER BY: LESLEY GEORGE

Father, I pray for the strength of women. When we feel low and apprehensive about our placement in the world, and when the world gives women unsolicited and unwelcomed opinions about who we're supposed to be in this world, I pray that you bring us to a place of intentional focus on you.

Lord, I pray that women—ladies and girls—would know how our future is so bright and full of purpose because our God made us with intentional purpose. Our past mistakes gave us experience, and we're still here because of the unwavering strength you put in us. I pray that women would know how unstoppable we are because you help us take every next step to move forward. Lord, help us remember that we're stronger than we know.

Lord, I believe in your strength, and I pray that women would believe in your strength until we find strength of our own. I believe in the strength of women because I know how you made us champions. You helped us go through unimaginable situations that would have broken others. You allowed us to experience things and have testimonies to share with the world that could be somebody else's healing. A woman who decides she won't quit in the name of Jesus has already won! Amen!

Scriptural reference: Jeremiah 29:11

# Disabled Children

PRAYER BY: PINKIE FARMER

Lord, thank you for the children who are disabled but are precious in your sight. Thank you for caring for them and making ways for them to be helped. You gave them abilities that have yet to be revealed. Help them push those abilities forth until they can be seen. Whatever the hindrance, help them be successful. Help them smile as they fight to overcome their difficulties. Let their surroundings be peaceful, loving and filled with caring people. Bless them with encouragement to keep moving forward. Father, when frustration invades their spirit, enlighten them with the smile of your countenance and your peace. Lift them up in your presence. Give them the courage to try again as you hold them up. Let them see themselves through your eyes and let them know your goodness.

Father, strengthen their ability to understand, and show them ways of doing things. Open up ways for them to function when it seems impossible. Lead them to places where they can use their minds and skills. Shine forth in them, O God, as the new day in those things they achieve. In those moments of disappointment, help them move forward. Lift them above the obstacles they face. Hear their cries and answer them quickly, O God. Where they need knowledge and understanding, provide it to them. You are their help and strength, O God. Remember their parents and all who help the children. Give them the wisdom, knowledge, and spiritual understanding needed for every situation. Thank you, O God, for hearing and answering this prayer in Jesus' name. Amen.

# Love

PRAYER BY: KEEVA DEDEWO

Lord, you are love. You, God of heaven and earth, Creator of all mankind, are the One who formed mountains and rivers and seas, and who spoke life into existence. From the beginning of time, you demonstrated your love for mankind. You performed the ultimate act of love by sending your son Jesus Christ to the cross so that he would die, be buried and rise from the dead to give eternal life to everyone who believes in you. You continue to show us the magnitude of your love—how wide, and long, and high, and deep it extends—that we may be filled with the measure of your fullness. How great is your love! How awesome is our God! Lord, thank you for being the example of how we are to love one another here on earth.

Father God, show each one of us how to love in our daily lives, and give us the fortitude to be faithful in our efforts. Teach us how to be patient and kind with one another at all times. When we feel jealous or are inclined to elevate ourselves above others, teach us humility so that we would not envy, boast or be proud. Give us the strength to lift others up so that you will increase, as we decrease. Keep us from being easily angered, and fill us with grace so that even when we are justifiably hurt, we would keep no record of wrongs. Pour your Spirit of love upon each one of us so that we would rejoice in truth, and not delight in evil. Lord, show us how to protect always, trust always, hope always and persevere…always. Replace the hate in this world with your love. Fill us with your love.

Lord, guide those who are looking for love in this world. Lead them to you first so that by finding you, they would find the true love they seek. Restore faith to those who are jaded and have given up on love. Renew hope in those who have loved and experienced hurt, pain and heartbreak in the process. May your love within us continue to grow and blossom with each passing day. Lord, thank you for your love. Amen.

# High Blood Pressure

PRAYER BY: ZANDER ALLEN

Heavenly Father, I come before you asking you to heal everyone with high blood pressure and let them know good health. Father God, I know that you're a healer and your word will never fail us, glory to God. It's your will for us to have good health. No one can stop you from blessing us. Father, you're awesome, you're merciful, and there's nothing too hard for you. Hallelujah, Father, help us eat the right foods to stay healthy. I rebuke high blood pressure IN THE MIGHTY NAME OF JESUS. Father God, your son Jesus Christ took all our infirmities and bare our sicknesses. Hallelujah, I thank you in Jesus' name.

Father God, I know we will be made whole. You're always standing with us, glory to your name. It's your will for us to have strength. We put our faith in you. We know you won't fail us. You brought us from a mighty long way. Father, I thank you for our healing. Yes Lord, we claim your healing in Jesus' name. There's no one like you Father. You're so wonderful, you're so great, and you give us newness every day, glory to God, hallelujah. Without your mercy upon us, we don't know where we would be. Father God, I thank you for all these things that I came asking of you in Jesus' mighty name. Amen. Amen, and amen.

Scriptural reference: Isaiah 53:5

# Pro Athlete Moms

PRAYER BY: WANDA WRIGHT

To the most High God, I come to you with an open heart and in faith. I'm asking you to watch over all NBA moms and their families. Guide and protect them. Watch over their sons so that they keep their eyes on the goal, staying humble and being team players. Have mercy on their health and keep them out of harm's way. Father God, keep your arms around them and block people who don't have their best interests. Oh, I know you are a forgiving God, but you see all and hear all. I believe in your word and know it works in your time, not ours. Father God, I ask that you watch over the ones in the NBA and the ones on the way to the NBA. Cover them and their families with your armor. I pray that their families get the knowledge and understanding of you to keep them away from all negativity. Place your light in them so they can shine through good times and bad. I ask these things in your name, Father God. Amen.

# Faith

PRAYER BY: JESSICA FRANCOIS JOHNSON

Hallelujah! Thank you, Jesus! Dear God, I come to you as boldly and as humbly as I know how. Father God, we know faith is a gift from you and we thank you for it. In your word, you said faith is the substance of things hope for, and the evidence of things not seen. O God, we trust and we believe your work, even when we don't feel it or see it. You tell us in your word that you're a God who doesn't lie. Father God, you said in your word that heaven and earth will pass away, but your word will continue to go forth forever. Wherever I'm lacking, wherever your people are lacking, LORD God, we ask you to give us the Spirit of faith. Lord Jesus, we need you more than ever before

Lord, you tell us in the word of God to trust you. We trust you in all we do. I'm calling on your name for your people in the world, O God, to speak things in faith that we know we haven't seen yet. We believe you will heal the land, O God, because there's power in the name of Jesus. We thank you in advance, O God, for what you're doing and for what you're about to do in all our lives. LORD God, we thank you for who you are. I pray this prayer for the people of God. I decree and declare it to be so in Jesus' name. Amen.

Scriptural reference: Proverbs 10:12-13

# Colon Cancer

PRAYER BY: APOSTLE DINA HUBERT

Father, I first want to thank you for healing me from stage four colon cancer in Jesus' name. I give you all glory, honor and praise for showing yourself mighty and strong, but Father, I now stand in the gap for the hundreds of people who have been diagnosed with colon cancer. I pray that their hearts and minds, Father, will not go into panic. Lord, send your comfort and reassure them that you're Jehovah-Rapha, our Healer. With you, nothing is impossible for them that believe, and that nothing—absolutely nothing—is too difficult for you. Father, I pray you be with them through a process that can be so scary and overwhelming. I pray you be with them during their operations. I pray you give them clarity when it's time to decide whether to choose chemotherapy, or radiation, or both. Lord, be there to cancel the voices of fear and the enemy telling them of their imminent death in Jesus' name.

I pray that you be with them when they lose their hair and assuring them in how they're fearfully and wonderfully made. Guide them to the right doctors who will educate them of all the choices they have to combat this dreadful sickness in Jesus' name. Lord, strengthen their loved ones who have to endure the process with them. Encourage wives and husbands in dealing with their own emotions at the same time they have to support their spouses who were diagnosed. I that pray you strengthen their families and friends as support systems for every colon cancer patient in Jesus' name.

I pray that awareness and early detection will spread rapidly. I pray that people will listen to their bodies and get themselves checked whenever they see their health deteriorating. I pray that schools and churches find it needful to educate on the signs and symptoms of colon cancer in Jesus' name. I pray that you guide your servants into the hospitals and minister to cancer patients, assuring them that with your stripes, they're already healed. I pray your hope and love is spread to each patient they encounter, some of whom have no family or friends visiting them.

I pray and believe one day you will release a cure for all cancers in Jesus' name!

# Relationships
PRAYER BY: PASTOR RHONDA BOLDEN

Father in the name of Jesus, I ask for your supernatural love to live, to dwell, and to intervene in every relationship across the land. May there be peace within our walls and prosperity in our palaces. Without you, O Father God, life has no meaning, so I pray that you become the center and foundation of every relationship. Let fathers and sons, mothers and daughters, sisters and brothers, husbands and wives, employers and employees, co-workers with co-workers, pastors and lay members, and every other relationship come together!

May the fruit of the Spirit, the Golden Rule, affection, appreciation, and recognition live and exist in the daily fiber of every marriage now in Jesus' name. We speak against confusion, condemnation, stubbornness, arguments, rage, anger, division, disrespect, abuse, belittlement, financial stress, lack of affection or intimacy. We call every marriage blessed, happy, healthy, wealthy, exciting, full of love, peace, and joy in the Holy Ghost. True appreciation and gratefulness are the order of the day in each home in the land now!

No longer will co-workers mistreat and plot against each other, and no longer will family members not speak to one another because of past hurt. We declare, decree and apply the blood of Jesus to cover every hurt and every pain now in Jesus' name. Father, heal hurting hearts now in Jesus' name! No weapon formed against these loved ones will ever prosper, for your Word says that a kingdom where people fight each other will end in ruin and a family that fights will break up! Now Father God, we thank you now for happy, heavenly husbands and wives, for happy, heavenly homes, and for happy, heavenly communities in the land in the mighty and awesome name which is above every name, Jesus Christ our Lord. AMEN!

Scriptural references: Psalm 122:6; Luke 11:17

# Direction

PRAYER BY: ALLISON WILLIAMS

Dear Father, we come to you seeking direction for our lives. God, this world we're living in is complicated, and sometimes the path we need to take is tough to navigate, but we believe that you have a greater meaning and purpose for our existence. We are in perilous times where sickness and division are pulling us apart, and now, more than ever before, we feel lost. So we turn to you for guidance and direction. Even as we plan for our future, our desire is that our plans line up with yours because we know that you know what's best for us.

Remove every roadblock from our path, and even with chaos looming around us, help us keep our hearts and minds on you. Help us not to look back and rest on past accomplishments or continue to relive past failures that might hold us back. You admonish us to forget about our past and to stop going over old history, but instead to be present and alert for the new things you're about to do through us. Help us to be focused, ready, and open to the move of your Spirit.

Lord, we realize that while we often operate in hindsight, your vision is 20/20. You see all, you know all, and you desire to lead us to an abundant and prosperous life if we trust you with our goals. We can't see the big picture and sometimes we put limits on ourselves and on you, but you are a limitless God. You've had our plans mapped out long before we were created, so we forge ahead in faith knowing that we are being guided by the Master and our steps are ordered, even when we aren't completely certain about the route we're taking. When we're unsure, we ask you to give us peace. When we feel lost, set us straight and illuminate our path. When all we see are impossibilities, open our spiritual eyes so we can focus on what you promised to do. You promised to direct our path, to give us strength to endure hardship, and make a way where there is no way. Help us to rely on your strength and not just our own. Help us to trust your wisdom and not just our understanding. Above all, in everything we do, may we be salt and light to the world around us. Amen.

Scriptural reference: Isaiah 43:18-19

# Wrongfully Incarcerated

PRAYER BY: PASTOR RACHELE A. DIXIE

Lord God, the Giver of mercy and hope, we pray now by your great power that you look upon all who have been wrongfully incarcerated. Father we pray that you cover them with your grace and shower them with your hope. Change their mindsets and the mindsets of those around them. For those who feel that they have lost their lives, give them a sense of purpose beyond their present circumstance. Provide advocacy and resources to them that will help them be free from cares of this life and give them greater life through their testimonies. If they believe in their minds that there is no way out, God we pray that you open up doors seen and unseen. Bring situations and people into their view to encourage them to be hopeful and not settle for their circumstances. Show them a place of comfort. Show them that there is something beyond where they are today.

We renounce this cycle of criminal justice system blindness that allows these unfair situations to occur in our cities and our communities. We ask you to raise up men and women who will be a voice for the ones wrongly accused and convicted. We ask you to release resources that have been held back. Prick the hearts of those who have more than enough so they might be compelled to give out of their abundance and speak out for those who have no voice. Form new connections that will be stepping stones for those trapped in this situation. Release people from the fear that has them bound and causes them to believe that they will not know a better life than what they have.

Lord, break this cycle in the name and by the blood of Jesus Christ. We believe you for the innovation and means by which these men and women will see release and find new life. Restore hope to the hopeless and bring help to the helpless, for you Lord are great. Provide ALL that is needed to the wrongfully-incarcerated so they will have new life in Jesus' name. Amen.

# Poverty

PRAYER BY: JUANITA WALTERS

Father, I pray that your people whom you have chosen from the beginning of time understand that you are Jehovah Jireh. I pray that we put you first in all things and allow you to be the epicenter of all that we do. Help us to seek your wisdom and discernment as we become financially fit and walking in the overflow. You are our provider and you shall meet every spiritual, emotional, physical, and financial need of every believer. Your word tells us that you will meet all our needs according to the riches of your glory in Christ Jesus. You are our shepherd and we shall not want. You are the well that never runs dry, therefore, we understand that lack will not be our portion. You are our source and we shall be good stewards over all that you place in our hands. We will tithe and pour into your storehouses.

Father, help us to become good stewards of our gifts, talents, resources, and finances. Help to understand that little becomes much in our Father's hands, therefore, we put all our hope and trust in you. I pray that we understand the power of sowing into good soil in the right season. Poverty will not be our portion. We will create generational wealth and legacies for future generations. We will walk in obedience to your word. Father, form our mouths to speak abundance into existence! Thank you for blessing the works of our hands so that we may walk in overflow and that you may be glorified!

Scriptural references: Matthew 6:33; Proverbs 28:27, 3:9-10; Psalm 24:1; Matthew 25:2

# Fear

PRAYER BY: LINDA M. JOHNSON

Dear God, I pray against the spirit of fear
  No more fear of darkness
  No more worry, for all our troubles are over
  No more sleepless nights from predators, child molesters,
  rapists; aggressive men are far from us

Dear God, I pray against the spirit of fear
  No more fear of speaking up and speaking out
  No more suffering from our past lives of sexual abuse
  No more sleepless nights from nightmares waking us up
  in terror from threats because we revealed what our
  abusers did to us

Dear God, I pray against the spirit of fear

# Asthma

PRAYER BY: DAWN HILL

Father God, today I come before you as one of your devoted servants, interceding on behalf of your people as they struggle with asthma and other breathing conditions. God, I'm asking you to breathe life and strength into their lungs. Strengthen their bodies so they can continue to worship you and spread your good word. Help the ones who struggle to make it through the day with coughs and pains and every issue that asthma causes. We ask you to stand with that child in gym class who wants to be able to play like their fellow classmates. We ask you to stand with that wife who's not able to do her errands without struggling in her breathing. Help those whose dreams are restricted by this roadblock. God, please touch their bodies. If there's any sin or wrongdoing that they're doing knowingly or unknowingly doing, please show them and guide them.

Father, help them realize that you're the one and only true Doctor, and that your will is for us to believe and trust all your decisions. Allow them to use this condition as a testimony to draw others to you. Help them realize that you haven't cast them aside, but that you've chosen them as disciples to follow you. Father God, show them that there's praise, blessings, and glory in this path where your children might have some struggle and pain. Strengthen not only their lungs, but their spirits as well. Lord, help us be steadfast in your word and find comfort in you. I ask you to please clear their minds of every foul thought they may have. Show them that we're made in your image and for your glory. Father, we thank you for what you've already done, and we thank you in advance for everything you're going to do in our lives in Jesus' name. Amen!

Scriptural reference: Genesis 1:26

# Doctors

PRAYER BY: DESRENE OGILVIE

Most righteous heavenly Father God, today we stand in the gap on behalf of those at the forefront in the field of medicine. Jesus, throughout various centuries and cultures, you blessed us with doctors who spent long, tedious years learning how to promote, maintain, and restore our health. You gifted them to learn how to diagnose and treat diseases, injuries, sicknesses, and impairments. Father God, these earthly healers took the sacred Hippocratic Oath before you to study health and promote healthy living. Father, they made the vow before you, the most holy and highly-esteemed Great Physician, who gifted them with knowledge, wisdom, and understanding to help your greatest creation live longer and healthier lives with quality. God, as we lift up these men and women dispersed throughout the earth, we pray that they treat their patients to the best of their God-given abilities.

We pray that they provide good medical care, compassionate bedside manners, and preserve their patient's rights to privacy. We pray that you encourage and strengthen their hearts from day to day so they would know they're doing a great work, and they would know they're fulfilling their special purpose and destiny to contribute to the betterment of mankind. God, we pray for medical students, residents, and interns to retain the necessary knowledge and skill sets being taught to them to advance to the next generation of physicians.  Father, we pray that you put your "super" on the natural gifts of senior doctors to share their experienced wisdom and insight concerning health and wholeness for this amazing creation you formed from the dust of the earth. Amen.

Scriptural reference: Luke 5:3

# Mindset

PRAYER BY: KENDRA RENEE' MANIGAULT

Dear Heavenly Father, in times such as these, we need to have a sound mind. We need renewing of the mind. I pray, and we pray, the scriptures over our lives for you to get the glory. God, I ask you to cover our minds to be sound to worship you all the days of our lives. Help us keep our minds stayed upon you! Keep our minds pure and clean for thy glory. I pray that you protect our minds as we put on the helmet of salvation.

Lord, keep our minds to stay focused on the things of God. Bless our minds to accomplish all the ministerial and spiritual gifts you've given us to do. Refocus our thoughts so we won't get distracted with the cares of this world. Empower our minds to move forward in destiny and purpose.

Cover our minds, Lord, to obey your will and your way. Let our minds be the same mind that was in Christ Jesus. Help us keep our minds stayed on Jesus and the Holy Ghost. We don't want confusion in our minds, because a double-minded man is unstable in all his ways. Lord, we thank you for covering our minds. Amen, and so shall it be in Jesus' name.

Scriptural references: Isaiah 26:3; Romans 12:2; Ephesians 6:17; Philippians 2:5, 4:13; 2 Timothy 1:7; James 1:8

# Drug Addiction

PRAYER BY: CELESTINE CISSE

Father in the name of Jesus, stretch forth your hand from above to rescue and deliver every drug addict from great, overflowing waters. Save them from the hands of every pharmaceutical spirit that mentally distresses and subverts your people. It is written in your word that you came to save the lost. Lord, you want all men to be saved and to know your divine truth. In the name of Jesus, pour out your mercy and love upon your people. Loose them from the awful bondage in which they are being held by the power of darkness. We command these evil, troubling and addictive drug spirits to go in Jesus' name. We break loose demonic oppression, bondage, witchcraft and cults; we denounce them in Jesus' name. You are the LORD who brought us out of the land of Egypt so that we should no longer be their bondsmen. You broke the bonds of every yoke so that we may walk uprightly before you. Let this scripture be fulfilled in our lives today. Let there be uprightness in Jesus' name.

Father, in the name of Jesus and according to your word, we hereby believe in our hearts and speak with our mouths that they come to know Jesus as the Lord of their lives. We pray that they confess that they are free and delivered from alcohol and drugs from this day forward in the name of Jesus. No longer can Satan harass or manipulate any unclean thoughts or habits of addiction in their minds, wills and emotions today in Jesus' name. They will not be the slaves of anything that exalts itself over the Word of God, nor will they be brought under its power again in Jesus' name. They are strong in the Lord to draw the strength to enable them to live free from the bondage of addiction today in Jesus' name. As an act of their will and faith, let them now receive complete and total freedom from their addictions. Let them be free and delivered today because they called upon the name of the Lord according to that which is written in your word. I thank you Lord, and. I praise you because they are now whole and redeemed from every evil work of addiction. Amen.

Scriptural references: Leviticus 26:13; Psalms 50:15

# Transition

PRAYER BY: SHARON FRANK

Dear Lord, blessed be your name! I worship you because all creation must praise you, for you are Lord! Since the beginning of time, creation has been called to be in harmony with you. In this season of transition, I pray that we remain in harmony and at peace with you. When the storms of life approach us, I declare that we will stay strong because you will fight for us. You will not leave us nor forsake us. Life can often be overwhelming when the environment around us changes, but I pray that we do not respond like the disciples did on the boat during the storm. During transition, I pray that our first response will not be "Teacher, do you not care about us?", but rather, "Teacher, we will not fear because you are with us!" I declare our peace to be still during life's transitions.

Just like the disciples were in awe of your authority at that moment, we find comfort in knowing that you reign forever and ever. Even in times of transition, you reign. New beginnings can be a scary thought. New territories can be uncomfortable places. Uncertainty can often leave room for doubt, but we pray against these things in Jesus' name. We choose to acknowledge that you are the God who is in control of all things. You are in the heavens; you reign as King of all the earth and you do as you please. As we reflect on the many changes that we have experienced in life, the one thing that remains is you. You, O Lord, remain forever. Your throne is from generation to generation! In times of transition, I pray that we cling to your Word because heaven and earth will pass away, but your Word will not! Your word will stand forever, so let your Word continue to equip us and your Spirit continue to speak to us. We will continue to live by your Spirit so that we may be continually guided by your Spirit through periods of transition. Holy God, please continue to guide us and be with us so that we can cope and be made strong during this time of significant change. Thank you, Lord. Amen.

Scriptural references: Psalm 150:6, 47:7, 115:3; Exodus 14:14, 15:18; Hebrews 13:5; Mark 4:37-39; Lamentations 5:19; Matthew 24:35; Galatians 5:25

# Perseverance

PRAYER BY: VIDA WILLIAMS

Father, refresh our minds, and souls, our strength, and our faith in you. Help us, Lord, to pray with your perfect will in mind. Teach us some of the different ways to invite you in everything we say and do. We must learn not to give up even though the road gets rough and bumpy. Show us how to use your word as a guide. We must learn to use our disappointments and failures as learning tools as you taught us to do. God, we're in debt to you for giving us the gift of your only Son Jesus. Jesus is our joy and Comforter. Through our works and deeds in everyday life, we can become true disciples for you. God, we know you walk before us in the midst of our severe pain and suffering. You said you will never leave or forsake us. We must rest on your word. We must be thankful to you. Lord, we ask to have patience with us as you guide us day by day. We sometimes grow weary and want to take matters in our own hands. We must learn to lean on you and tarry just a little while longer. We give our prayers to you and we leave there them.

Father, we ask for your help with our decision-making process. Remind us to come to you first. When we get scared, please reassure us of your presence. We must not only lean on you but sometimes we want to fall into your arms. Sometimes we want to pray and we don't know what to say. God, we know you that you know our hearts and minds. You are our all and all. In times like these, it's so easy for us to give up. Give us the will to persevere because we need you more and more every day. Heavenly Father, thank you. Amen.

# Anger

PRAYER BY: APOSTLE LYDIA WOODSON-SLOLEY

Father, we come humbly before your throne of grace, asking for forgiveness. We know that life offers many challenges, and we're asking you to help us adjust to our present conditions and keep our hearts free from anger. Let your abounding grace overtake us. Cause us to recognize and receive the power of your grace in order to remain emotionally stable in the midst of our circumstances. LORD, it's hard to accept the reality of change, as well as accepting truth when things come to an end—even in death—but according to YOUR HOLY WORD, we can choose to find our resting place in the sovereignty of perfect will.

LORD, help us capture the supernatural reality of anger and refuse it from resting in our bosom. We don't want to be recognized as a fool in your sight or in the sight of others. LORD, we don't want to live in regret or despair. We want to walk in love. Therefore, we lift our hearts to your and we ask you to wash us in the blood of the Lamb. Cleanse us from all unrighteousness in JESUS' matchless name. Amen.

Scriptural reference: Ecclesiastes 7:8-10

# Single People

PRAYER BY: NINA D. BROWN

One seat, one view, one glass, but the vision is set for two. Two visions, two dreams, with one voice.

O Lord, gather our souls and lead us to the altar to tell our truths and speak our fears as we share our pain and the unknown desires of our hearts.

Do you hear our hearts wrestling with the pain of our past? while our dreams echo the reality of our failed choices? Please don't let the pressures of this world triumph over us as we hasten to you to find our purpose during this process of identification.

Lord, enlighten us and grant us strength according to your heart's desire. Guide our feet as we walk through our thoughts to understand the joy and gladness that awaits us at our seat for one.

O Lord, as we surrender our hearts and place them into your hands, we'll rest in you while you remove all traces of our past; our pain, let downs, regrets, abandonments, rejections, heartbreaks, and lies that silence the testimonies of our suffering. Please pardon our voices as they reveal our unresolved brokenness.

Please grant us the strength to await your instructions because it's a struggle to remain consistent in this uncomfortable space. Daily we seek your face as our souls move to humble our flesh despite the demands of truth to justify our position.

Cover our hearts, guide our tongues as you strengthen our faith and give us grace to endure. Not understanding your timing, we bow in submission as you cover us with your kindness. Lord, order our steps. We give you our trust as we wait at our table for one. For we are confident that as we wait on you, you will grant us your and our hearts' desires. Amen.

Scriptural reference: 2 Thessalonians 3:16

# Childhood Sexual Abuse

PRAYER BY: KANDRA ALBURY

Father in the name of Jesus, thank you for the spirit of the courageous conqueror of childhood sexual abuse. Despite the deep-rooted that she has endured, she is still standing. I speak to every place in her life that has been violated. Father, I pray against perpetual feelings of guilt, shame and self-blame. I bind those feelings right now in the matchless name of Jesus. I loose a newfound sense of peace, freedom, wholeness, and fearlessness.

The question of "Why?" will no longer torment her mind. I decree that she will step into the place of wholeness. I declare that even past abuse will work for her good and for your glory in Jesus' mighty name! The heaviness of the secret is no more. Even in this trauma, God, you will make good on your promise of healing. I'm expecting it and so it is! Depression and sadness shall be no more. I decree and declare that she will not make an excuse to be bitter and sabotage her blessings. Father God, do not allow her past to haunt her because she is free in the mighty name of Jesus. You are Jehovah-Rophe, the God who heals, and we believe this to be so!

Father God, may you heal this conqueror so that she becomes an ambassador of change, courage, and hope for others who experienced physical, mental, and emotional scars of childhood sexual abuse. In due season, may she be led to testify of her healing and deliverance! May conquerors arise in every nation to expose childhood sexual abuse and bring forth justice. We are change agents designed to shift the paradigm from brokenness to wholeness in Jesus' mighty name.

Sexual abuse is an attack of the enemy designed to steal our birth identities and create social ills such as teen pregnancy, addictions, and sexual promiscuity. You created us to prosper and be in good health, even as our souls prosper. May mental and emotional healing be this conqueror's portion. May she rise from the ashes of her past and walk boldly into her destiny as a new creation in Christ. Allow her life to be a picture of beauty and holiness. Send perverted thoughts of her self-worth into the abyss, never to return. Teach her to love and trust. May she also forgive her predator and others responsible for her pain in Jesus' mighty name we pray. Amen.

Scriptural references: Isaiah 61:1-3; Romans 8:28; Jeremiah 29:11; 3 John 1:2

----------

*This prayer is featured in Kandra Albury's memoir*
*"From Food Stamps to Favor" 8th anniversary edition.*

# Salvation

PRAYER BY: BILLIE OGLESBY

Father in the name of Jesus, we pray for your call to salvation to every man, woman, and child in the farthest corners of the earth. We pray for them to have open hearts to receive you as their Lord and Savior. We declare that the knowledge of truth would become a reality for them, and that they would know the price you paid for all of us to have eternal life. Father, we trust that the hearts and minds of those who never heard of your divine saving power will be reached, that scales would be removed from  their eyes, and the applied blood of Jesus would go beyond their minds into the depths of their hearts.

We pray that no one is beyond your reach. We declare that your people who share the good news are filled with compassion, mercy, and your unending love. Father, they'll know that their steps are ordered. They'll no longer be deceived and held captive by the cares of this world. We thank you for the Spirit of truth and wisdom who will reveal who you are as our Savior. In Jesus' name, the unadulterated gospel will be shared in a way that they'll not be able to refrain from your divine intervention. They will awaken to righteousness and serve the King of kings and the Lord of lords. Thank you for covering them with the blood of Jesus so they won't get weary. They will awaken to your righteousness to serve the true and living God and experience your sustainable grace.

We decree that you're the Lord of the harvest who puts laborers in the path of lost souls.  We call them from the north, south, east, and west. They will have the courage to set themselves apart from sin by your power. Your word says they will come to their senses and escape from the snare of the devil who held them captive to do his will. Lord, we speak divine design for every soul. Your God-given mandate will be fulfilled because salvation belongs to you. Lord, we won't be forgetful. We'll be intentional and diligent encouragers when we're prompted to share the good news of salvation. Most assuredly Father, your word says that by your grace are we saved through faith; it's not of ourselves, but it's a gift from you. Lord, we thank you for being vessels for your kingdom, and for being willing and available to do your will. We are so thankful for the mighty weapon of prayer in Jesus' name, hallelujah! Amen.

Scriptural reference: Ephesians 2:8

# Trust

PRAYER BY: PATRICIA ETHEAH

Hallelujah, we praise your name because your name is a high tower. Lord, we love you. You are the beginning and the ending. You are our Abba, our Father, our all-in-all, and our everything. We will always maintain our ways before you. Lord, help us to trust in, lean on, rely on, and have confidence in you. God, you are our refuge in the time of need. We thank you Lord, because we look up to the hills where our help cometh from. Our help cometh from the Lord, and without you, we can do NO good thing. Help Lord, we cry out to you for direction. We want more of you and less of ourselves. Lord, show us how we can trust and believe in your word. Lord, when we meditate on your word, it brings comfort to us. We're holding on to you so we can be overcomers through you. God, we have confidence in you to wait on you. You will show up for us. Whether your answer is yes or no, you will answer.

Lord, thank you for accepting our pleas. Thank you for loving us, taking care of us, and delivering us when you did. We love you for the promises given to us to trust, to stand, to move forward, and to perform what we know we have no strength to do. It's because of your word that we trust we can do all things through the strength of the Lord. Nothing is impossible with you. No good thing will our Father withhold from us or forsake us of because you love us. You gave your Son so that we can have eternal life. We experience and trust your love working in us and through us. In Jesus' name, we thank you for today. It's a new day and our hope is increasing because of our trust in you. We can say that better days are coming. Hallelujah, praise your holy name. Lord, teach us your ways. We yield our will to yours. We decrease so you can increase in us. Thank you Lord, for allowing us to learn to trust you through your word. By faith will we walk and also trust in your word. Amen.

Scriptural references: Job 13:15; Psalm 62:8; 125:1, 37:3, 143:8; Isaiah 26: 4; 2 Corinthians 1:9; Isaiah 50:10; Proverbs 3:5

# Abandonment

PRAYER BY: GLORIA FONDJO

Father, we often wonder, thinking that we're all alone. When life gets hard, we tend to think that we're on our own. We wander in the empty streets and cry our hearts out. We seek people's love and attention in order to feel valuable in this world. We get lost amongst the likes, the hashtags, and all the vanity that surrounds us. Father, your word says it all. We're never alone. Not for a minute, and not even a second passes by without you being by our side. We're valuable. We're important. We are enough. Abba, help us remember that we're never without you. Help us remember that you're with us and within us. We invite you to take your place back in our lives. We may have walked away from you and feel lost right now, but we cry out to you.

O Father, take your place back in our lives. We invite you again to be the Master of our lives so that even if family and friends turn their backs on us, we'll never feel alone. We're in you, and you're in us. Even when life gets hard, we'll always remember that you haven't and never will abandon me. You gave our only Son to die on the cross for us. We believe and declare that no weapon formed against us shall prosper. You're continuously fighting unseen battles for us. Father, the world can abandon us but as long as we have you, we'll rest in peace. In Jesus' name we pray, amen.

Scriptural reference: Isaiah 49:15-16

# President of the USA

PRAYER BY: APOSTLE MARTHA GREEN

Heavenly Father, we thank you for this day that you made. O Lord, lift up the president and keep him safe from all harm. We pray that he leads the people the way you want him to lead. Keep him in perfect peace and keep his mind stayed on you. We thank you for the grace and mercy bestowed upon him. Lead him in the path of righteousness and keep him from all harm and danger as he travels to and fro. Amen.

# Dementia

PRAYER BY: ANTIONETTE LESLIE-HOLLAND

Dear Heavenly Father, I come to you in the name of Jesus. Father, so many of your children are stricken with dementia. It steals their precious memories. It affects their thinking skills and abilities perform everyday activities. Although man says there is no cure, Lord, we know you make the impossible... possible. We are guided by your Word that all things are possible with God. Lord, you know how difficult it can be for us to see family members not remembering how to do simple things and not remembering children's names. Father, I pray for those who have been stricken with this disease. Lay your hands on all those affected by dementia. You alone have the power to heal. Touch the hands and minds of every doctor, scientist, specialist, researcher, and all medical personnel involved with finding a cure for dementia. Father, I thank you in advance for divine healing. I thank you for the many medications that were invented to slow down the progression of dementia.

I thank you for those who donate money towards the cure. Lord, I trust you, I believe you, and I believe there will be a cure for dementia. Your word teaches us to wait for you. I know our time is not your time and I know you are always an on-time God. So many have succumbed to dementia, but Lord, my faith is in you because you are victorious. You are mighty. You are an awesome God and this battle against dementia will be won in the mighty name of Jesus, I pray! Amen!!

Scriptural reference: Matthew 19:26; Psalm 27:14

# Firefighters

PRAYER BY: MINISTER TYRA FRAZIER

Gracious and kind Father, we honor and we praise your name. We thank you before we ask for anything, O God. We reverence your holy and righteous name. We give you glory and honor and we thank you for your presence, O God. Lord, we come on behalf of your children, specifically every firefighter throughout the land. We pray now for a hedge of protection over their lives. We pray for covering as they travel to and from to assist people. God, we pray for your grace and mercy to surround them. We ask that as they cover and protect their bodies, that you O Lord would do just the same. God, we pray that you give them clarity of mind, perfect vision, and wisdom that exceeds their years and training. Allow them to see in the Spirit and have their every move be targeted and specific to the call they are answering. Give them supernatural strength needed not only to carry their protective gear, but also to carry people to safety.

God, I pray that you keep them in perfect peace. Guard their hearts and minds, O God. Don't allow them to take their work experiences home, nor what they see to their families. Don't allow the things of the world to overtake them, but give them reassurance and hope that they are making a difference in the lives of those they serve. Guide their footsteps, O God. Your word says the steps of a good man or woman are ordered by you. Order their steps, God. Keep them from danger seen and unseen. Protect their vision so that they see clearly. God, protect their hearts from excessive sadness and heartache. Protect their lungs from the constant smoke they inhale and give them the physical agility to perform their jobs to the best of their abilities.

Direct them to perform their jobs without bias or discrimination, but with love, compassion, empathy and concern. In the name of Jesus, I pray. Amen.

# Politics

PRAYER BY: MOZELLEN DOBIE

Thank you, Jesus, for your goodness and your mercy. Jesus I give you the honor and the glory. Thank you for your grace, hallelujah! Thank you for allowing us to come to the throne of grace about the confusion in politics. I pray the politicians acknowledge you in all their ways. I pray for their unity to be with one accord. I pray for the mind of your people. God, give them clarity of thought. I pray for the government to turn from its wicked ways and seek you. Jesus, I ask you to help them make good decisions for your people. Thank you Jesus, hallelujah. Help politicians realize that if they take your name out of government, they are lost. Jesus, you are the head of government and you put people in positions to serve. Hallelujah! Jesus, you are good to us. You are the great I am. Hallelujah! God, I glorify you because you are faithful to your people.

Jesus, your word lets us know a house divided cannot stand, and that includes the White House. I pray for the president, the Senate, and House of Representatives to come together with a one mind to do your will. I pray that the name of Jesus be in every mouth and upon every lip. I pray that their hearts be turned to you. Jesus, I bind pride and confusion and I loose humility and clarity of thought. Jesus, I bind the devil and loose the blood of Jesus. The word of God is true. The government is upon His shoulder, and God has the authority and the last word. Hallelujah! Jesus, I bless you because you hear and answer the prayers of your people. I pray that your will be done on earth as it is in heaven in Jesus' name. I stand on your word and it never fails. Jesus, you promised never to leave us or forsake us. Your word is life in Jesus' name.

Scriptural reference: Matthew 5:4

# Identity

PRAYER BY: VERNETTA DRUMMOND-MERCER

Father God in the matchless name of Jesus, we come humbly before your throne asking you for forgiveness of our sins in thought, in word, and in deed. We bless your name and we thank you for the divine purpose that you assigned to our lives. Thank you for creating us in your own image and for hand-picking us. We are grateful that old things have passed away and that you are doing a new thing for your people. We glorify your name and ask you to exemplify yourself through our identities. God, you have blessed our lives by ordaining us to be a chosen race, a royal priesthood, and a holy nation. Thank you for choosing us to be a people for your own possession. Father, through your love and kindness, we appreciate that you have given us identity as your children. What we will be has not yet been revealed, but when you appear, we shall be like you. Lord, we desire to reflect you. We thank you for giving us gifts that have been tailored for our identities. God, we ask you to continue revealing your agenda to us and within everything we do. Let it continue to reflect your love. We ask you to continue to receive the glory and lifting up your standard within us.

We exalt you, O Lord. As we abide in you, we pray that your perfect will continues to abide in us so we may continue to bear good fruit within our identities. Without you, we are nothing. As we take up our crosses daily and follow you, as we sacrifice our agendas to trust you, we submit our minds, our bodies, our souls, and our spirits for your specific use. We thank you for your saving grace and the new life brought forth through your purpose of promise in us. Your word says that those who are led by your Spirit are the sons of God. Thank you for casting off the spirit of bondage designed to keep us in our old identities with the fear and sin of the world. We are now your sons and daughters for whom we cry Abba! Father! We are truly grateful to know that as your chosen ones, you granted us the ability to put on compassion, kindness, humility, meekness of character, and patience. You now move within us and you help us to walk continuously in your likeness. When everything else failed us, and when we had no clue of who we were and what we are worth, it was your love that gave us the strength and ability to fight and know who we are in you. Amen.

Scriptural references: Genesis 1:27; Proverbs 25:2

# COVID-19

PRAYER BY: DR. LESLIE DUROSEAU

Dear God we cry out, we love you, we need you. Hear our prayers O Lord. Answer our petitions. How many more of us must die? How many more shall become sick? We are desperate. We sing hallelujah, hallelujah, hallelujah, we give you the highest praise.

There is dis-ease across the land. To whom do we turn? We turn to our Creator, the one who created all things well. Lord, hear our cries and our petitions. Do not let us go down to *sheol*. Come and rescue us, for there is great distress. A pandemic has come and invaded us. We are locked in and locked out.

We thirst for you as a deer pants for water. Quench our thirst and feed us dear Lord, till we hunger no more. We thirst and hunger after your righteousness, for your justice and peace in the land. Pour out living water upon the people and the land that will satisfy and supply all our needs. Our souls long for you in the midst of such trial and tribulation.

Where does our help come from? Indeed, our help comes from above. Our help comes from the Lord. Dear Lord, be our refuge and our help in this ever-present time of trouble. You, Lord, are near to the broken-hearted. You are always near those whom you love.

Come Lord, and save us once again. Save us from ourselves, for you alone are our Comforter and our strength. Amen.

Scriptural references: Psalm 46:1-3, 8-11

# Women

PRAYER BY: TENARIA DRUMMOND-SMITH

In the precious name of Jesus, I come before you Lord, asking that you will bind that spirit that has women not liking one another for no good reason. I ask that you release the spirit of love and kindness to rain on every woman in the world. Lord help us to respect ourselves in order to respect others. I ask in the mighty name of Jesus that you bind that spirit that has women betraying one another because of their own insecurities. O God, help women learn how to complement each other without any false pretenses behind what they say in the name of Jesus. Lord I ask in your name to help us celebrate each sister in her season of blessing and to understand that you will do the same for us in the name of Jesus. Lord, you are a God who will bless whom you will bless at any given time.

Hallelujah, hallelujah, I thank you Lord, thank you Jesus. I ask you to help us lead by example so the younger women will know that it's important to carry ourselves like ladies in the way we dress, speak, and in how we respect other women. Lord, help us learn how to call and check up on another sister when she might be feeling down. O God, help us learn how to listen when a sister just needs someone to talk to. Lord, I ask you to help us to pray for someone who is going through, even when we don't find ourselves getting along with them. Help us to have the heart to pray for them in the name of Jesus. Lord, I surrender this prayer unto you in Jesus' name, and it is so. Amen, and amen.

Scripture reference: Philippians 2:1-2

# Parents

PRAYER BY: SOPHIA L. GREENE

Father, we ask you to come at our call because you chose our wombs to use as vessels to expand the world. We never received a manual...or did we? Teach us how to raise your children. Give us your patience and show us your way. We cannot raise these children without your protection, guidance, and courage. You are the Father of all nations. We are the caretakers of these souls. We lay all the children of the world at your feet because we acknowledge that you word is the manual of the world and in your word, we can find the answers to help us to be good parents. Thank you, Abba.

# Dementia, Alzheimer's Disease

PRAYER BY: ROBERTA JONES-JOHNSON

Hallelujah! Lord, I worship you Lord, and I give you all the praise. I thank you for giving me life today. Father, I lift up your name. There's nothing I can do without you. Please forgive me where I fall short. You're the great God, the God above all, the King of kings, and Lord of lords. I give you all the honor and the glory!

Father God, I come to you in the mighty name of Jesus, interceding for those suffering from dementia and Alzheimer's disease. Some of our loved ones are affected by these diseases. We watch as they move a little slower and speak less than they did before. They have difficulty remembering and recognizing people and places. They find it difficult to recall treasured memories that are fading away. We see the wondering in their eyes. They used to participate in the world, but now they're shut out and look at the world from the outside.

Lord, I ask you to cover them in the blood of Jesus. Please be with them, bless them, and heal them. They're still loved by you and are precious in your sight. I pray also for their caretakers. Father, please comfort them and give them strength to cope with the challenges of caring for their loved ones, who once knew them all so well and now appear to be strangers. Be with them as they struggle with confusion, mood changes, memory lapses, helplessness, and frustration. Encourage them and add patience to them as they care for their loved ones. You're the Father of grace and mercy, so I ask you to help them show grace and mercy as they support their loved ones.

Father, let your Kingdom come to deliver us from all the diseases and illnesses we face. You said in your word that there will be a new heaven and a new earth. There will be no more death, or sorrow, or crying, or pain. You said that these things will pass away, so let it be so in the mighty name of Jesus. Amen.

Scriptural reference: Isaiah 65:17

# Divorce

PRAYER BY: PROPHETESS VON BRAND

Father, I lift up those today that have faced divorce and still struggle with the pain from it. I come against the spirit of rejection, whether through fear of rejection or self-rejection. You remind us that you did not give us the spirit of fear, but of power, love, and of a sound mind. I bind those spirits of bitterness, depression, unforgiveness, retaliation, and anger. I command the strongman of guilt and shame to loose their hold. By your Word, we can do all things through you that gives us strength.

Lord, I thank you for showing us that there is hope in you. We are not discouraged, but are encouraged because we know that you are our sustainer. You and you alone, God, are the lifter of our heads, so we give you glory and we give you all the praise. You are our Jehovah Jireh; you will make provision for us and our households. We break the backs of every soul tie that has come to hinder us from our future, and we cast them into the dry sea. We uproot every plot and plan of the enemy to rob us of our joy.

God, we yet thank you that we're not moved by this temporary state that we're in because there is a future for us. With or without a spouse, we stand on your Word! We thank you for your Word and for your peace today. You are faithful, glory to God!

Scriptural references: 2 Timothy 1:7; Philippians 4:13; Psalm 42:5

# Family Dysfunctionality

PRAYER BY: ANNETTA DRUMMOND

Father in the name of Jesus, we honour you, we praise you, and we glorify your name. Thank you for your grace and mercy. We thank you for the families that we were born into because you have created and sanctioned families from the foundation of the world. You placed us into families for your praise and glory.

Some of us have good families, but some have dysfunctionality that needs your healing and deliverance. Father, we ask you to go the root of dysfunctionality in our families and bring order where there is chaos. We know that you can make something beautiful out sadness. Father, we ask you to touch the parents, children, relatives and friends in these homes. Bring about stability, structure, joy, peace, and most of all, shed abroad your love into their hearts. Touch those who are broken and shattered. Let them know you love them unconditionally.

Some father or mother has lost their son or daughter to the streets. I pray that you provide a safe place for them. Protect them, cover them under the blood of Jesus and bring them home to their families and loved ones. Release the pain of those who are contemplating suicide. I ask that you send your angels to intervene and save them. Let them know they are loved, wanted, and can be used by you even in their broken state. I ask you to bring peace into their situation.

Father, I pray for abusive parents. God, I ask you to go to the root of their abusiveness and heal them of all hurt and pain that they went through themselves. Meet them in that dark place holding them captive, angry, and making them lash out. Set them free to release their hurt to you. Let them know your healing in this life in Jesus' name.

Father, I ask you to restore long-lost families. Bring home the absent father and turn his heart toward his family and children. I ask you to touch and heal every dysfunctionality in our families around the world. Heal, restore, reunite and deliver in Jesus' name. Amen

# Politics

PRAYER BY: QUEEN MOTHER

O Lord God, we call on you to help the politicians who help govern our lives to make decisions that are clear and wise. We pray for our leaders' righteousness, O God. We pray for our leaders to work with us in our dealings in society. Sustain us in all our ways. Let us endure in your divine mercy and grace. Help us to be mindful of each other as we live in community as neighbors looking out for one another. Give us the leadership of men and women who will seek their guidance from you, the Supreme Leader of all things at all times.

Hear us, God who art in heaven and on earth. We ask you to awaken true leadership in our leaders. What more can we ask of you, but that our leaders turn to you and you alone for guidance in every decision they make on our behalf? O God, our leaders make decisions affecting our lives from birth to death. Hear us O God, show us your way as we ask you to lead and guide our lives. Help our leaders to be righteous in all their decision-making. Help us to sustain our communities and live in harmony with one another. We thank you for all things. We thank you for hearing our humble prayer and accepting it. Amen.

# Unforgiveness

PRAYER BY: JANET LENNOX

Hallelujah, thank you Jesus, we come in the matchless name of Jesus giving thanks and praise to who you are. Father, we ask you to forgive us of sins that we have committed against you most of all, Lord, and against our children, parents and friends. Lord, we need our prayers to be heard by you, therefore whatever sin we have hidden in our hearts, please forgive us so we can experience your grace right now in Jesus' name. Our lives need to grow, so unforgiveness cannot be part of our lives.

We look forward to life more abundantly. Lord God, let the fear of you always be with us so we will have your forgiveness in Jesus' name. We thank you for the work of the cross, and we thank you for wholeness in the matchless name of Jesus. Let the blood of Jesus wash our minds from unforgiveness so we can prosper. Let the blood of Jesus come against the spirit of unforgiveness that dries up our lives from success and greatness in you. Heavenly Father, we thank you for our great success in you in Jesus' name. Amen.

Scriptural references: Psalm 103:10-12, 130:3-4

# Cancer

PRAYER BY: DAWN GRANTHAM

Father God in the precious name of Jesus, I come before you as your humble servant, asking you to hear my cry as I seek thy face. You know so many people have lost loved ones from this deadly cancer disease and so many are still fighting it. Doctor visits and radiation, chemotherapy has taken over their lives. This disease affects the people who suffer from it and their loved ones. Some have won this battle and others have lost it. My heartfelt prayer is for you to heal those who suffer and comfort their families who watch their loved ones suffer. Father God, I speak life by the power of my tongue.

Cancer has to flee in Jesus' name! It must go back to the pit of hell where it belongs. It doesn't belong in our bodies. It is not of good, but of evil. This disease has no age or race discrimination. It shows up ready to rumble and brutally attack our bodies. O Lord, I know this disease is not of you because it is wicked and monstrous. Therefore O Lord, I come boldly and approach the throne of grace, decreeing and declaring our bodies to be healed right now. Cancer, flee in Jesus' name! Lord, please raise up the sick from their bed of affliction and be their doctor in the operating room. Dry up cancer cells and remove every tumor growing in their bodies. Close up open wounds and help every organ function properly. To those who lost their hair, restore their hair healthier and longer than ever before. To those who lost their voices, restore them without the need for devices. To those who lost physical features and might not look like they used to, restore a glow to them so that when people see them, they will know that Jesus touched them. Do it for them Father

God, not because of who I am, but because of who you are. I come to you interceding on their behalf. Be their medicine and help them live a healthy lifestyle. Move on their behalf Father God. Give them the courage not to fear, and the strength to be a living testimony that Jesus still heals, Jesus still restores, and Jesus still performs miracles. I pray this in the precious name of Jesus!

Scriptural references: 2 Chronicles 7:14; Proverbs 18:21; Isaiah 53:5

# Grief

PRAYER BY: MIRANDA RIVERS

O Lord, our God and our Savior, I ask you to watch over all those who are grieving and comfort them. Send your angels of mercy to alleviate their sorrow. Father God, I ask you to take away their anguish and heal their broken hearts.

I ask that you comfort all their mourning family members. I ask that you uplift your people during their sadness. Give their weary hearts rest and still their minds with your peace. Help them to remember your promises to never leave or forsake them in their time of need. Help them to know that your presence will bring peace to their souls.

Father God, send your Holy Spirit to bring them peace and courage to live for you. Restore joy to their souls; uplift them, fill them with your joy so that they may flourish in hope. You know their pain and grief. I ask that you bless them with your peace in the midst of their grief and comfort their weary hearts. Give them hope in their turbulence, so that they can look to your love to sustain them in their time of need. We ask all these things in Jesus' name. Amen.

Scriptural references: John 14:27; Psalm 18:2

# Purpose

PRAYER BY: SARAH NICHOLS

Our God, we call you Abba, Father, because you're the one and true living God. You're the Maker of all things seen and unseen. You know the end from the beginning and you make all things perfect in their time. We adore you and we love you. We thank you for your purpose and plan for our lives. Your word tells us that you called us a chosen people, a royal priesthood, and your special possession. You had a special purpose for our lives. We're grateful that you chose us, and we want to follow you as you lead us and guide us to the purpose and plan you have for us. You placed all that we need to fulfill that purpose before us. Let there be light on our purpose, just as you spoke in the beginning and framed the world so that things that were not were brought forth. Father, you tell us in your word that you know the plans you have for us, to prosper us and not to harm us, to give us a hope and a future. Thank you for your great love for us.

Sometimes when we don't love ourselves, you show us how you planned a future for us and give us something to hope for. Where our hearts plan things that are out of your will, let your purpose for our lives be brought forth. Let us live for your purpose so that when we finish this race that is set before us, we'll be empty and have accomplished all that you gave us to do. We know all things work together for our good because we're called according to your purpose. As we walk on the path you've set before us, you said you would fill us with joy in your presence, and with eternal pleasures at your right hand. May the Holy Spirit stir up the gifts and talents in us so that we may know what you put in us and show us what we need to complete our purpose. Send us the people you've assigned to us and our purpose. Give us the discernment to know who they are and how they'll help fulfill your divine purpose in our lives. We give you glory and honor for what you're doing and for what you've already done in us, even before the foundation of the world. In Jesus' name, Amen.

# Community

PRAYER BY: CAMEO BOONE

Our Father in heaven, I come to you in the name of Jesus, lifting your name on high. I thank you for the opportunity to come to you in prayer on behalf of communities all over the world, especially the black community. Father, our community is filled with violence, prostitution, drug dealing, addiction, greed, poverty and dysfunction. Our children are suffering from a lack of structure and education. The enemy has set up shop in our communities and is fixated on our children. We, as the church, can create a structure and use our spiritual weapons to knock down the strong holds of satan. He has no authority over our communities, and he has no power over our communities! We use the precious gift of the Holy Spirit to break every yoke of the enemy!

Your word says to pray without ceasing and that's what the spiritual leaders and the followers of Jesus must do. Father, we know in your word that you sent angels when Daniel prayed and fasted. You softened the heart of King Cyrus and he let the Israelites free. We know through our trials and tribulations that you would never leave or forsake us, that if we humble ourselves and seek your face, you will heal the land. Thank you, Father, because you hear our cries and prayers and are coming to deliver us.

Thank you, Father, for your hedge of protection around our communities. Thank you for preparing a way for your people to come out of this system, to live righteously and self-sufficiently. Thank you for making a way for us to build our own houses, to have our own businesses, and to create our own school curriculum so our children will know structure and truth! Thank you for moving us to implement your word and prayer into our curriculum. Thank you for showing the family, school, church and community how to work in concert to nurture one's gifts so their talents will provide for them, and not just toiling away at a job. Thank you for raising up leaders who will help lay the foundation to your Kingdom by making disciples who will build communities all over the world that serve you. Amen!

Scriptural references: 1 Thessalonians 5:16-18; Daniel 9; Ezra 1:6; 2 Chronicles 7:14

# Judgement

PRAYER BY: CYRINTHIA HILL-FLOWERS

Father in the name of Jesus, we can clearly see that your judgement is in the land. There are many situations that allow us to see your power in the earth. Father, you have said in your word to believe so that we are not consumed and condemned by sin, because the wages of sin are death, but the gift of God is eternal life through Jesus Christ our Lord. Jesus, we don't realize that things are happening because of constant disobedience. The times are evil and things are happening because we will not take heed and change our ways.

Father in the name of Jesus, I decree change in the lives of people. I decree and declare that people will believe and accept you. Lord Jesus, I pray that they will know you for the pardon of their sins, that when they face God's judgement and stand before Him to be judged, they will have a record that they pleased God for being obedient to his word. Jesus, your word declares that he that believeth on him is not condemned, but he that believeth not is condemned already because he hath not believed in the name of the only begotten son of God. Jesus, help people believe that you are a rewarder of those that constantly seek you. It is not your will that any should perish, but that all should come to repentance. Lord, you sent your Son Jesus not into the world to condemn the world, but that the world through you might be saved. Help us, Jesus, to be very careful of the words that we speak. Lord, every idle word we speak, we shall give account thereof in the day of judgement. For by thy words, thou shall be justified, and by thy words thou shalt be condemned. Lord, help us to watch our words and be very mindful of the words we speak in Jesus' name. Help us to know we will be judged. Help us to make our calling and election sure in Jesus' name. Amen.

Scriptural references: John 3:17-18; Romans 6:23, 14:12; Matthew 12:36-37; Hebrews 11:6; 2 Peter 1:10; Revelation 20:12

# Low Blood Pressure

PRAYER BY: JOYCE ROLLINS

God, we're so unworthy to come before your throne, yet you hear our petitions and send the answers we need.  Father, I bless and magnify you. I thank you for victory over sickness., and I give you the glory. I thank you for the authority to intercede on behalf of those who suffer with low blood pressure. God deliver them! I won't stop praying until they 're totally delivered. I look to the hills from which comes our help. I know our help comes from you, and I know you have all power! God, send your healing power for your people to be healed.  I call on the name of the Lord, who is worthy to be praised. Lord, I send up a mighty praise to your name for what you're about to do.

Lord, I ask you to heal low blood pressure. I come against low blood pressure in the name of Jesus. Father, right now I speak against every cause of low blood pressure; stress, allergy, heart disease, anemia, neurological disorders, old age, poor diet, Injury and dehydration. I place sickness under my feet. I proclaim victory over every symptom. I speak to nausea, tiredness, confusion, palpitations, unsteadiness, fainting, dizziness, and lightheadedness. I command you to cease in the name of the Lord Jesus. Today, I proclaim that Illness is no longer our portion. A healthy lifestyle is ours; we shall live, and not die. I proclaim miracles, signs, and wonders on our behalf. I even speak that the doctors will become saved after witnessing our healing. I pray that in our healing, we'll experience fullness of joy that comes only from the Lord. God, I've seen you do it before, so I'm asking you to do it again. God be our healer, our strength, and our source. Help us to lean on you in the time of need. Lord, surround the sick with people who love them. Cover them as they go out and come in. Be a shelter until their healing is complete. God, touch every doctor that they meet and give them knowledge to treat your people effectively. Lord, increase their faith in the name of the Lord Jesus. The doctors will treat your people, but you are the healer. God, you continue to get the glory, the honor, and the praise. I'm thanking you in advance for your people, Lord. Amen.

Scriptural references: Psalm 121:1, 18:3

# Wisdom

PRAYER BY: CHERYLN OLIVER-McKAY

Heavenly Father, I come to you asking for wisdom for each and every one in this world in the name of Jesus. Oh God, we're living in the perilous times that your word speaks of. There is no clarity, and so much judgment. Your people are lost without you Lord, and we need your wisdom. You said in your word that if any lack wisdom, they should ask you, who gives generously to all without finding fault, and it will be given to them. Lord, your people need your wisdom. They're confused and are making wrong decisions. We know your word tells us to be careful about how we live, not as the world lives, but as the wise, making the most of every opportunity because the days are evil. God, we know that you are not the author of confusion. Lord God, you said in your word that the fear of God is the beginning of wisdom. We pray for people to fear you, not to be frightened of you, but to open their minds and hearts to receive you. Lord, we need to know that you are guiding our every movement. Help us to remember that nothing in this world compares to your wisdom.

The wisdom that comes from heaven is pure, peace-loving, considerate, submissive, full of mercy, fruitful, impartial and sincere. Help us remove our thoughts so we can see what you're showing us. We live in a world that seems too loud, too noisy, and too busy for us to hear you. Lord, raise your voice in our souls so we may hear you and have the will to be obedient. Lord God, we know that it's better to have wisdom than gold, so it's with this prayer that I ask you to have mercy on everyone. Let those things that you have for us be revealed. Lord, I pray that we receive the wisdom that comes only from you, and have the discernment that we need in these last and evil days. I pray these things in Jesus' name, amen.

Scriptural references: James 1:5; Ephesians 5:1-16

# In-Laws
PRAYER BY: ESTHER BURGESS

Heavenly Father, I come before you thanking you for the grace to come boldly before your throne and to bring before you every matter of the heart. Father, I thank you for all you have done for us. I thank you for the blessing of having a family. As you have given the command to multiply and inhabit the earth, we thank you for the union of marriage and the extension of our families. Lord, you know and understand the joys and testing of marriages, and the disruption that arises when there are differences. Holy Spirit, I present every daughter-in-law, every son-in-law, every mother-in-law and every father-in-law before you. I ask that you intervene in every area of our relationships, giving us a heart to love, to forgive, to have patience. Help us to accept the things we cannot change so that we might know how to communicate and show forth your love in all that we do. Help us to love past every negative judgement that may arise in our relationships Help us to let go and forgive every negative word said in error and every inconsiderate action done.

Guide us in the things we do. Give us the wisdom to know when to speak and when to be quiet. Humble our approach towards negative in-laws so that by our fruits, you will be glorified. Teach us how to bring everything to you in prayer. I pray for every spouse who feels inadequate because of the negative criticism their in-laws speak towards them. Give them strength to overcome. Give us the wisdom how to deal with difficult in-laws and teach us how to handle every difficult task. Holy Spirit, restore and redeem in Jesus' name. I pray for every unsaved in-law. Holy Spirit, work upon their hearts. Give them the heart to surrender and bring them to repentance and salvation. I pray for the grace of God to come against every resistant heart and every spirit that comes to hinder the union of family. I pray that love will grow stronger in our relationships. I pray we will be able to love as you do in Jesus' name. Amen.

# Children

PRAYER BY: THERESA BYRD

My God, I come to you in pray knowing that all things are possible through you. LORD, our children today are caught up in this lost generation. Their mindset is beyond the unthinkable. The streets are calling their names and children are answering the call. Children with no supervision are out here causing harm to others. They're disrespecting their elders and innocent people. All the morals and standards they were taught no longer exists for them. In their minds, it's okay to rob, steal, and rape their elders. They're not learning anything, and the ones who have children aren't teaching their children anything. It seems like self-destruction is their top priority. So many innocent children are being bullied and losing their lives over nothing. Parents don't know what to do or where to turn.

Father God, you're the only one who can put an end to all this mess. I pray, LORD, that you bind the evil thoughts that these children share with each other. Help them be responsible enough to correct another. For these things I pray, and I'm thankful for the blood you shed on the cross at Calvary for all of us. Amen.

Scriptural reference: Proverbs 3:5-6

# Backbiting

PRAYER BY: PASTOR SHAWN QUALLO

Lord, we come now rebuking the spirit of backbiting out of the kingdom of God, out of our homes, out of our workplaces, and out of our schools in the name of Jesus. Your word tells us that the spirit of slander is a hater of God, insolent, arrogant, boastful, inventor of evil, and disobedient to parents. These things are present because a door was opened to the spirit of backbiting. We uproot every seed planted from backbiting. We call forth the fire of God to consume slander, hate insolence, arrogance, boastfulness, evil inventions, and the spirit of disobedience. We drive them out in Jesus' name. Lord, every tree you did not plant, we uproot right now out of the hearts and minds of your people. Your word tells us to put aside all malice, deceit, hypocrisy, envy, and all slander. We repent now Lord; forgive us for allowing the doors to open in our hearts and minds. Holy Spirit, we invite you into our hearts and minds because we receive you Lord, you tell us to cast our cares upon you because you care for us. Help us to stop fighting our own battles and know that you are a very present help in our times of trouble.

Lord, your word tells us that the mind is the battlefield, so we bind and cancel the spirit of lying that entraps our minds. We destroy it now in Jesus' name and we loose the spirit of peace, joy and love that are the fruits of the Spirit. We loose them to saturate our minds and hearts through the blood of Jesus. Now Holy Spirit, cause our eyes to open and our mouths to declare a sound that the spirit of backbiting is destroyed. Let love abide, because love covers a multitude of sins! Lord, thank you for the love that will be manifested in us as we walk in forgiveness for those who backbit us. No weapon that forms against us shall prosper. The enemy seeks to devour us, but we reserve every demonic angel to chains of fire for everlasting punishment now in Jesus' name. We put on the whole armor of God, and the spirit of backbiting can no longer dwell in us. We proclaim that we are redeemed and our minds are renewed in Jesus' name. Amen.

Scriptural references: Romans 1:30; 1 Peter 5:7; Ephesians 6:11-13

# Grace

PRAYER BY: JACQUELENE SCRUGGS

Heavenly Father we thank you for another day. Thank you for this day that we have never seen and that we will never see again. Thank you, Jesus, for our life, our health and strength. We thank you for the shelter over heads and the food on our tables. We thank you, Jesus, for being our Savior, our Father, our King, and our everything. Lord, you mean everything to us. You are so good to us and we thank you for your love and grace. We are not perfect, but we don't claim to be perfect. We are striving to be like you. We thank you for the grace you have stored in us. We have all power in Jesus' name. Lord, you are so good to us and we can't live without you.  We thank you Jesus, glory hallelujah. Lord, we thank you for everything.

Lord, your grace and mercy brought us through. We live in this moment because of you. We thank you and praise you for all things. Jesus, we thank you for what you are doing and what you are going to do. You give us hope every day because we know that your grace is going to give us strength to face life's journey. Father, you are worthy to be praised. We thank you for the power of Christ resting upon us. Lord we thank you, glory hallelujah, you are awesome. We love you Jesus. Glory to your name. We thank you for saving us, blessing us, and keeping us by grace through everything we go through. We thank you, Lord, for the Holy Ghost that abides in our souls. Your grace and mercy is enough for us because you are always there for us. Jesus, we thank you for never leaving us or forsaking us. Lord, you are good, and your mercy endures forever. We love you and are forever grateful to you. May the grace of the Lord Jesus

Christ and the love of God be with us all. Amen, Thank you, Jesus.

Scriptural references: Ephesians 4:7; 2 Corinthians 12: 8-9

# Man of God

PRAYER BY: WENDYANN WILLIAMS

Lord, I lift up the men who have a personal relationship with you and whose heart's desire is to get to know you on a deeper level. Please allow them to have the mind of Christ so they'll think like you and honor you by putting you first in their lives. Help them to always remember to wear the helmet of salvation so they can make wise decisions to guard against the negative thoughts of the enemy. Allow them to see with spiritual eyes that the battles they face are not against flesh and blood. Their battles against their past, their weaknesses, their shortcomings and insecurities. Let them see how the enemy uses these things against them so they may always wear the full armor of God to withstand the attacks of his enemy.

Help them keep their eyes focused on you so they will know how to turn away from temptation and seek you for deliverance. Protect their ears in what they hear so they'll only hear from you and know your small still voice in the midst of all noise and confusion. Help them choose their words wisely so they'll be pleasing to you. Lord, may their speech always be free from perversion and be uplifting, gracious, and astute, so that others may want to get to know you. Protect their hearts from evil desires and deception and show them how to look to you as the source of direction and strength.

Guide their footsteps wherever they go so that they'll be pleasing to you. Show them how to walk humbly in your grace and with godly countenance so your character may be an example to others. Most of all, show them and help them know how much you love them. I pray this prayer in Christ's name, amen.

Scriptural references: Ephesians 6:10-17; Colossians 4:6; Psalm 19:14

# Cancer

PRAYER BY: SHERRELL D. MIMS

Jehovah Rapha, God our healer, we approach your throne of grace on behalf of your people with our arms outstretched unto you. We pray that this foul spirit of cancer does not attach itself to your people. We sever that assignment at the root and throw it back into the pit of hell from whence it came, never to rear its ugly head again. Right now, Father, we continue to stand on your word. You saith that no weapon that is formed against us shall prosper, and every tongue that shall rise against us in judgment we shall condemn. This is our heritage as servants of the LORD, and our righteousness is of you.

Jehovah Rapha, we thank you for bearing our sicknesses, diseases, and plagues so that we may endure healthy and prosperous long lives. Every promise that you made to us is "yes" and "amen". We stand on your promises. Jehovah Rapha, you are the great physician! You can do anything but fail. We consider it done in Jesus' name. We seal this prayer, knowing that you heard our prayers and will answer them. We praise your holy name, Jesus Christ our LORD and Savior. Amen, and so be it.

Scriptural references: Isaiah 54:17, 53:5; James 5:16

# Parents

PRAYER BY: D.D. HOUSTON DUPREE

Dear Lord, as I lay here in bed in the quiet of the night with an open heart and sound mind. I don't go to church as often as I should, but I call on you every day. I can't stop thanking you for the awesome woman that you gave me in my mother. Children are so blessed to have encountered a lifetime of love, support, patience, friendship, encouragement, guidance, and just plain mental and spiritual togetherness. We thank you for giving us the patience and frame of mind to listen to our moms' advice. What would our lives be like if we didn't? Lord, we thank you for being able to honor our moms with love, respect, support, and obedience. This is what you expect children to do. Lord, you showed us how to make our moms happy just by listening to you.

Lord, we thank you for a loving experience that can't be compared to any other relationship. We praise you, dear God, for giving us a phenomenal gift that no amount of money could replace. I pray that our youth will honor their parents and realize that the support and love they receive from them are unmatched. I pray for those children who don't have a loving relationship with their parent(s). I pray for those children to get on their knees and ask for the help of the Lord. I pray that our youth find a place of worship to show them how to mend broken relationships with their parent(s), I know if we look for the love of our Heavenly Father to solve a problem, the problem is already solved. Thank you, Lord. Amen.

# Incest

PRAYER BY: JEAN THOMPSON

My glorious God and Savior, I awake this bright morning to give you thanks, honor, and all the glory. You're worthy of all the praise for watching over me, my family, and the entire world. God, you do all this because you love us so much. My Lord you're consistent and you never fail in all that you do. When we slumber, you're working on our behalf and letting us know we have nothing to fear. Your name is highly exalted above every name, and you're worthy above anything we could ever ask for.

Lord, I stand in the gap praying for every situation and circumstance of incest. I pray for every man, woman, boy or girl who had incestuous acts done toward them. You know the heart of the ones who suffered, and you know the heart of the ones who made them suffer. Jehovah, our Redeemer, you gave up your life so we could live. Through dangers seen and unseen, you watch over us even through this wrongdoing.

Master, Son of man, show us light in this dark and dreary world. We share your goodness with the world to let people know you're waiting to hear from them. We cry out for the healing of the heartbroken. We cry out for their deliverance. Man might be able to fool man, but man can never fool our God. Emmanuel, we pray that incest will never be a heartache that families have to endure. Father, be in our midst always. Amen.

Scriptural references: Genesis 19:32-35, 29:16-35; Leviticus 18:7, 20:11-21; Philippians 3:13-14

# Brave Space

PRAYER BY: LESLEY GEORGE

Lord, I pray for the human race to have a common understanding of one another as we share this common existence on earth. I pray that we would be kinder to each other, and gain understanding toward each one's culture and religious beliefs.

As women, I pray that we show compassion to one another as we travel through this life. There are so many people on the earth, yet somebody can still be lonely in the midst. During this COVID-19 pandemic, we are practicing social distancing from one another, but this does not mean we should be in isolation. Checking on family members, neighbors, and church family members shows our vulnerability in caring for them, and at the same time, creates a brave space for them to confide in us. They might not have the courage to open their hearts and discuss the things hindering their growth potential.

Lord, show us how to create a brave space—from a safe space—for women to release the vail of guilt and shame. Emotions and past circumstances can sometimes keep us stuck in the past and keep us from looking forward to our amazing future. We don't' have to ask "What if?", or "Should I?" Father, we have a purpose because you gave us a purpose. Every day is a blank slate that we're blessed with to make a new start. Father, help us find hope, creativity, and love in abundance each day. Amen.

# Attitude

PRAYER BY: PINKIE FARMER

Help us, O God!! The uncontrollable feeling of anger is worse than an engine releasing steam! Our release hurts others verbally and emotionally. You're the Almighty God who's able to change anyone of us. We come before you in desperate need of your help. We yield our will and our way to you. There's nothing too hard or impossible for you. You can melt our heart of stone and make it kind and lovable. Be our help, O God. Forgive us for the outbursts, the backlashes, and the misunderstandings we've caused. Forgive us for accusing, for hating, for hurting, for rejecting, and for denying out of anger. Forgive us for the bad feelings, harsh attitudes, jealousy, and any other problems we caused because of our behavior toward others.

Wash us in your Spirit, inside and out, and make us clean. Through your power, we expect and receive a new attitude. We forgive others for everything done to us in the past, present, and future. As we release them from these incidents, we let your peace abide in us. They're free, and so are we. Bless them with good health and prosper them in their endeavors.

Lord, we thank you for each day as we allow anger to fade under your power. We think peaceable thoughts to replace angry thoughts. You guide our feet and direct our steps. We thank you because we're unable to do this on our own. Lord, you're mighty and powerful. Thank you for helping us overcome anger in the name of Jesus. Amen.

# Family

PRAYER BY: KEEVA DEDEWO

**77**

PRAYER

Dear Lord, I thank you for the gift of family and for the blessings you bring to families worldwide. I pray for your continued blessings upon families throughout the world – those produced through bloodlines and those produced by human choice. Lord God, please move within each and every family and address their most pressing needs. Provide healing and forgiveness to families that are hurting and in pain. Bring peace to families that are in turmoil. Reunite families that are dispersed. Provide wisdom and guidance to families that are lost or confused. Provide resources and address the physical and emotional needs of families that are lacking. Move within our families. Replace hate with love, pain with healing, and bitterness with joy. Restore families to be sanctuaries of love, support, and community.

Lord, while we do not choose our birth families, you hand-select every person who enters our lives to be there for a reason and a purpose. Thank you for those whom you have placed within our families. Install strong and Godly matriarchs and patriarchs within families to provide leadership, wisdom and direction to our children. May they share the message of God's love, so that it permeates lives for generations to come. Send your angels of protection to watch over our children and shield them from harm. Show mothers and fathers how to train up children in the ways of the Lord, and teach them how to parent effectively.

Father God, remind us that even in moments when we feel we are alone or lacking family in this world, YOU are our Father and the source of all good things. We trust you to meet ALL of our needs and provide family support for us here on this earth. May our families be centered and grounded in the eternal and unfailing love that comes from knowing you personally, truly, and intimately. Amen.

# Pastors

PRAYER BY: ZANDER ALLEN

Father God, I come before you asking you to protect pastors. Be a fence around them and protect them. I pray that you keep your pastors in righteousness. Give them strong minds to fight temptation all around. Lord, I trust you because you're the living God, and if there are any that are wolves in sheep's clothing, let them be revealed. It's so hard to find the right pastors who are really and truly doing the work of God. Father. let them be still and hear you speak to them quietly. Let them see all the goodness you put in them. Father, we all need to get it right with you. Open up our ears, our hearts, and our minds, hallelujah. Show your pastors that you're on their side and they they're not alone.

Father, I pray that your pastors' mouths be filled with the Spirit in their preaching from the pulpit. Let there be faithfulness in preaching the word of God to your people, hallelujah, bless your name. Father God, I pray for your pastors to have patience and grace with all people. I pray that your pastors create a welcoming atmosphere in the church and show love. Let your pastors' leadership, vision, and services be in accord with your will. Father God, I praise your holy name. Amen.

Scriptural references: Matthew 7:15; I Corinthians 10:13; Deuteronomy 31:6

# Homelessness

PRAYER BY: WANDA WRIGHT

Dear God, I come to you with my hands lifted up high, praying for the homeless people all over the world. Guide them to safety and give them comfort. Open up doors for them. Protect them from all danger. Make it possible for them to get to the right places so someone can help them. Open up the hearts of everyone who can help them. Let them feel your presence. I pray for compassion and mercy to all the people who have to face these difficult times. You said you are a merciful God. I know you have the power to change all things. I step out on faith and pray for all people who are homeless. Father God, I ask that you see them through. Amen.

# Fear

PRAYER BY: JESSICA FRANCOIS JOHNSON

Thank you, Jesus! Hallelujah! Lord Father God, I come to you boldly asking you to deliver everybody who deals with the spirit of fear. Father, your word tells us you haven't given us a spirit of fear, but of love, and power, and of a sound mind. O God, we know you haven't given us a spirit of fear because you want us to do things in faith. I ask that you touch our minds so we can do all that you've called us to do in the name of Jesus. O God, we know that spirit is nothing but the work of the devil to put in our minds that we won't be effective to do things for your Kingdom. Father, I cry out to you for your people. I bind that spirit of fear in the name of Jesus because you've given us power, love, and a sound mind.

LORD God, we need your help today in these trying times. We can't do anything without you. I plead the blood of Jesus, O God, that you will continue to help us. Keep us covered under your precious blood. I thank you for giving me a heart to push forward and move...even when that spirit troubles me. LORD God, loose your angels to war on our behalf so that we're victorious. LORD, you are exalted. I put all my trust in you because you said you give your angels charge over us. Thank you for being a good Father. You made us, you know all about us, and you know everything coming our way. We'll wait on you for everything. Amen.

Scriptural references: Psalm 91:14-16

# Family Dysfunction

PRAYER BY: APOSTLE DINA HUBERT

Father, I first want to thank you for healing me from stage four colon cancer in Jesus' name. I give you all glory, honor and praise for showing yourself mighty and strong, but Father, I now stand in the gap for the hundreds of people who have been diagnosed with colon cancer. I pray that their hearts and minds, Father, will not go into panic. Lord, send your comfort and reassure them that you're Jehovah-Rapha, our Healer. With you, nothing is impossible for them that believe, and that nothing— absolutely nothing—is too difficult for you. Father, I pray you be with them through a process that can be so scary and overwhelming. I pray you be with them during their operations. I pray you give them clarity when it's time to decide whether to choose chemotherapy, or radiation, or both. Lord, be there to cancel the voices of fear and the enemy telling them of their imminent death in Jesus' name.

I pray that you be with them when they lose their hair and assuring them in how they're fearfully and wonderfully made. Guide them to the right doctors who will educate them of all the choices they have to combat this dreadful sickness in Jesus' name. Lord, strengthen their loved ones who have to endure the process with them. Encourage wives and husbands in dealing with their own emotions at the same time they have to support their spouses who were diagnosed. I that pray you strengthen their families and friends as support systems for every colon cancer patient in Jesus' name.

I pray that awareness and early detection will spread rapidly. I pray that people will listen to their bodies and get themselves checked whenever they see their health deteriorating. I pray that schools and churches find it needful to educate on the signs and symptoms of colon cancer in Jesus' name. I pray that you guide your servants into the hospitals and minister to cancer patients, assuring them that with your stripes they're already healed. I pray your hope and love is spread to each patient they encounter, some of whom have no family or friends visiting them. I pray and believe one day you will release a cure for all cancers in Jesus' name!

# Entrepreneurs

PRAYER BY: PASTOR RHONDA BOLDEN

Father in the name of Jesus, I thank you for every entrepreneur from the north, south, east and west! I thank you for their tenacity in refusing to give up when business is slow, but I now declare and decree them debt-free and stress-free. Their businesses are blessed, their families are blessed, their workers are blessed, and their clients are wealthy and are blessed because they choose to do business with them.

New contracts are now being signed, new territories are being added to their lists, and business relationships are being established now! No longer will they experience times of decrease, but they will know INCREASE in Jesus' name. Lord, we know one may plant, and another waters, but you, O God, are the only one who can bring forth increase. May their businesses be a blessing to millions of people who need what they have. Let your favor open doors of opportunity that are shut. As you touch the hearts of men, let new opportunities be prevalent.

Lord, we pray for entrepreneurs' new divine connections and partnerships with organizations and successful business gurus so they can launch events, programs, and products to help others become entrepreneurs and do business for your glory. We thank you for the creation of new jobs from new businesses that shall come forth from new business partnerships! Lord Jesus, you told us in your Word to occupy until you come, so I pray that a spirit of entrepreneurship begins to raise up many across the land. May they create legacies for their families and increase their learning through books. So now, I decree and speak forth birth of business tycoons in real estate, fashion design, the automobile industry, technology, marketing, graphic design, the literary publishing industry, Internet industry, and television production.

Lord, we thank you now that money is no longer an issue in the lives of aspiring and current entrepreneurs ever again. They will have everything they need to do all that you divinely downloaded into their spirit to do with ease. They are mighty and massive money magnets in the mighty name of Jesus, and so it is.

Scriptural reference: Luke 19:13

# Loss

PRAYER BY: ALLISON WILLIAMS

Dear God, we thank you for the promise that even when we are sad or mournful, in time, joy will come. Father, we acknowledge that loss is an inevitable part of our lives and we all experience it in one form or another. Some of us have lost jobs or material possessions, and some of us are dealing with the devastating loss of someone we love. These experiences can bring on feelings of resentment, hurt, confusion, and heartbreak. Lord, in our lowest moments, help us find peace in the midst of the storm. When we find ourselves in a state of desperation, we will lift our hands and our circumstances to you as a sign of surrender. Not as an act of giving up, but in giving it all to you to you so you can work on our behalf.

Father, give us a shift in our minds and our perspectives. Help us realize that although our loss is difficult or even painful, our ability to heal and grow through it depends on how we view it. When we want to shut down, remind us that our hardships aren't just occurrences, but that they're in fact a part of our process. God, we acknowledge that loss can be devastating. We admit that, often times, we are resistant when you allow things that we want or love to be stripped from us. With our limited perception, it's hard for us to see that there are places you want to take us and things you want to do in our lives that require some type of loss and that sometimes we have to let go in order to receive greater from you. Shift our focus from the loss and give us fresh eyes to see and appreciate the gains that come through our loss. Despite our hurt, today we choose to place our trust in the God who is greater than any hardship we may face. Help us to accept your will, even when we don't understand it. When we're bent and close to breaking, cultivate strength in us that we didn't know we had. Shape us through our trials and turn our tests into testimonies for someone else who may be struggling. Give us beauty for ashes, joy instead of tears, and praise instead of despair. Amen.

Scriptural reference: Psalm 30:5, Isaiah 61:3

# Gun Violence

PRAYER BY: PASTOR RACHELE A. DIXIE

Holy God, your word calls on us to love our neighbors as ourselves. In this day Lord, we have seen far too many shootings against our brothers and sisters. In the name of Jesus, we bind the spirit of the world that causes people to justify this behavior, O God. We pray that the thoughts of those who rationalize gun violence be converted from evil thoughts to good thoughts. Restore the mind of Christ to your people, a mind that represents compassion, love, and peace. We are losing far too many people to shootings. We are seeing lives—from infants to the elderly—being negatively affected, touched by death or long-term debilitating injuries. God, you called your people to pray and we do so right now.

Let our voice be heard, and help us do things that will stop the gun violence from continuing. Help us create advocates who will not back away when evil voices try to combat them. Engender hope to all who have been affected by shootings. Help them know that you are the God who has the perfect plan. Help each of us surrender to that plan and trust you through the storms. Gun violence against your people must be quenched and we— as your people—will continue to rise above the tricks of the enemy. Lord, you are in control of all things. Therefore, we renounce gun violence RIGHT NOW. We speak love for our families, our neighbors, and our country in thought, word, and deed in Jesus' name. Amen.

# Rape

PRAYER BY: JUANITA WALTERS

Father, I come praying for the heart, mind, body, and spirit of every individual who has been violated sexually. I pray that you restore, rebuild, uplift, and remind them that they are loved by you. I pray that you roll away their shame, heal their pain, restore their reputation, and vindicate their honor. Father, help them understand that you have the power to mend and heal the broken pieces of their lives that resulted from sexual assault. I pray that you send the Holy Spirit to comfort them during those times when their tears fall, when flashbacks come, and when their emotions overwhelm them. Father, shield them from spirits of depression, oppression, shame, guilt, hopelessness, fear, insecurity, lust, sexual perversion, unforgiveness, and all unclean spirits that try to place them in bondage.

Father, set them free from bondage. Destroy the chains and yokes that come to hinder the power of your healing. Help them, Father, to forgive those who violated their bodies and minds. Help them to love themselves and see themselves through your eyes. Help them to use their voices and testimonies to speak life and empower others. Father, help them draw closer to you by studying and meditating on your word. I pray for them to have the peace that surpasses all understanding in the midst of their trials and tribulations. Remind them that all things work together for their good and that you will deliver them.

Scriptural references: Jeremiah 31:3-4 30:17; Exodus 15:26; Psalm 147:2, 103:2-3; Matthew 11:28-29; 1 Peter 2:24; Mark 5:34; Isaiah 54:17, 35:4; Romans 5:3-4

# Universe

PRAYER BY: LINDA M. JOHNSON

Lord, I pray for the universe and all creation
You are the one true living God
Planet earth strategically placed among the others in the galaxy

The bright sunshine, the mystical moonlight, and the stars that twinkle so bright

The earth is the Lord's and the fullness thereof, and they that dwell therein; Lord, you founded it upon the seas, and established it upon the floods

O God in heaven, the universe is crying out to you, desperate for a cure from this pandemic
Lord, I pray for the entire world, Asia, Africa, Australia, Antarctica, North America, South America and Europe. For every country, state, city, town, village, and every community.
Lord, bless the universe—from every mountainside and everything that exists at the bottommost of paradise, to every river that streams and every ocean you formed, and everywhere the human race exists on this earth—and bring the peace and tranquility that calms raging seas.

O Lord. our Lord, how excellent is thy name in all the earth. This is my prayer for the universe of every woman, girl, man and boy of every race, color, creed, and diverse tongue.

This is my prayer Lord –that you allow every believer who claims salvation to take their God-given authority to do as Jesus Christ did when He went about all the towns and villages healing the sick, raising the dead, and setting the captives free; even greater works shall we do. God, you said in your word that if we speak to that mountain of worry, doubt, fear, sickness sexual abuse, verbal abuse and poverty, it will move.

This is my prayer –that you will heal the universe. This coronavirus/COVID19 pandemic came to destroy mankind, but you are the One who holds the sparrow, you are the One who stands by us. Help us to remain strong and resilient, totally relying on you as we cry holy, holy, holy, Lord God Almighty, the Maker of the universe—the only wise God—who sent your only begotten Son. Jesus is the light of the world, and He wants us to let our light so shine. This is the prayer I pray for the universe.

Scriptural reference: 2 Chronicles 7:14

# Vision

PRAYER BY: DAWN HILL

Father God in the name of Jesus, I come today on behalf of your people. I pray on behalf of all who are physically and spiritually blind. Lord, your people are looking and lusting after things that are not of you, and causing their eyes and spirits to become blind to your light and to your way. Your people are focusing their eyes on worldly things and unholy living. Please help those who don't even realize they're being blinded. Father, I call on you in the name of Jesus because only you can heal the blind. Please touch their hearts and restore their spirits so they may be clean vessels to be used by you. O God, remove the scales from their eyes so they might not walk into darkness, but into your light and glory. I ask you again, Father God, to remove the scales from their eyes and allow them to find and walk in the path you created for them. Cleanse them, because you say that you won't dwell in an unclean temple. I'm asking you to restore their sight from spiritual blindness.

I pray for those who are physically blind. I'm asking you to strengthen them. They don't know whether their condition is permanent or temporary, but God, help them understand that you don't make mistakes. Help them realize that they're not loved any less than those who have sight. You love and watch over all your children. Help them understand the plan that you set for their lives Help them understand that, through your, they're able to do anything they put their minds to. Help them know they can still be used by you. Lord, strengthen them so they won't fall into depression. Strengthen them to live their lives in joy and peace. We thank you in advance for healing and restoring our vision, and for allowing us to glorify your name. Amen!

Scriptural reference: John 12:40; Psalm 146:8

# Afflictions

PRAYER BY: DESRENE OGILVIE

Most righteous heavenly Father God and Creator of every living thing, we come boldly before your throne of grace, asking you to have mercy upon your children. We ask you to deliver us from all our afflictions. Daddy God, you created us in your own image and likeness, and you breathed the breath of life into us to become a living soul. Your most prized creation was designed to be perfect and without infirmities. Our forefathers yielded to temptation and their disobedience to your mandates allowed sin to enter the world. Our immortal bodies became mortal, and our flesh knows pain, suffering, and affliction. We were born in sin and shaped in iniquity, but God we thank you for sending your Son Jesus to suffer and die for our afflictions. You said He was wounded for our transgressions and bruised for our iniquities. The chastisement of our peace was upon Him, and with all His thirty-nine stripes, we were healed. Father, we stand on that word and we believe your Word cannot return to you void.

You said we would have afflictions in our bodies. Although we may be battered and bruised physically, mentally, and emotionally, we turn our afflictions over to you.  God, although the pain sometimes seems unbearable, you alone are our balm in Gilead. You're our peace in the midst of the storm, you're our strength, our battle axe, our Wonderful Counselor, and our Great Physician. God, there is nothing that you can't heal us from or take the pain from.  Lord, we thank you for enduring the crushing and bruising for us. Our afflictions may hurt us, but you said you would deliver us out of them all, and not one of our bones would be broken. Even if you decide to take us out from this flesh, our spirits will be delivered. No more pain and suffering because we've been engrafted into the body of the resurrected Jesus, and we'll live blissfully in the peace and joy of heaven forever more. Amen, and amen.

Scriptural reference: Psalms 34:17-20

# Body of Christ

PRAYER BY: KENDRA RENEE' MANIGAULT

Lord, I pray for the body of Christ all across this land. You're the head of our lives. In faith, I pray that we stand in the Spirit of unity. I pray that we love each other as we've been commanded to love. We need to love from within the abundance of our hearts.

God, my prayer is that you continuously keep us covered under the blood of Jesus. Father, keep us day by day as we abide in you, and you abide in us. You're the vine and we're the branches. Keep us connected to you Lord, keep us connected so we won't stray. Lord, keep watch over the body of Christ! Keep us together and as one, with no jealousy and envy amongst us. I pray that the body of Christ will act as one because we're all members of this one body. The members are many, and though we're many, yet we are as one. We won't fight each other in the spirit realm, but we'll do all things in decency and in order.

We're the body of Christ, and by one Spirit are we all baptized into one body. Whether we be Jew or Gentile, whether we be bond or free; we are one. When one member suffers, all members suffer with it. When one member is honored, all members rejoice with it. We're members of your body, your flesh, and your bones. We're the body of Christ and we're here to please you Lord. Amen!

Scriptural references: Romans 12:5; 1 Corinthians 12:27; Ephesians 4:5, 5:30

# Whoredom

PRAYER BY: CELESTINE CISSE

Father in the name of Jesus, we thank you for giving us the keys to the Kingdom of heaven. We bind, plunder and cast out principalities, powers, the rulers of the darkness of this world, and the operation of spiritual wickedness in high places. Thank you for making your people on earth heaven-bound. Father, deliver them from the spirit of whoredom. In the name of Jesus, break every tie affecting their souls for the worse. We speak to every demonic power that has taken advantage of them. We pray against every sexually-impure spirit in their lives. Through your blood shed on the cross of Calvary, and through your wonderful name, we renounce all demonic soul ties known and unknown. Father, totally cleanse and make free by the outpouring of these words. Make free from this day forward and deliver souls from the works of the flesh. Satan, you and all your principalities, powers and master spirits who rule the darkness in high places are bound. Lord, loose the Spirit of holiness and sanctification in the name of Jesus. Strengthen and reinforce your children by the mighty power of the Holy Spirit who lives and dwells in them. Help them draw your strength to enable them to live free from bondage.

Father, raise up the standard of the Holy Spirit against every spirit of whoredom and sexual pollution. In the name of Jesus, every seductive spirit trailing their lives is bound, and every spirit of sexual abuse is destroyed. No weapon of whoredom formed shall prosper and every demonic tongue of whoredom is condemned. Holy Ghost fire, purge their lives in the name of

Jesus. Burn off every evil force and satanic power causing lustful desires in the children of God. They are made free and delivered because they call upon the name of the Lord as written in your word. Lord, we praise you for deliverance, and your children confess your anointing and transformation all over them. Thank you for their cleansing and forgiveness in Jesus' name. Amen.

Scriptural references: Romans 3:23; Ephesians 3:20-21

# Emotional Distress

PRAYER BY: SHARON FRANK

Eternal Father, you see our hearts and you understand our predicaments. We are not at rest, but we seek you during this period of pain. We seek you because you are our refuge and strength, an ever-present help in trouble. Your name is a strong tower where we can hide and be safe. Father, help us regain control of our emotions. Help us so that we no longer grieve, for the joy of the Lord will be our strength. We don't want to rely on ourselves. We want to rely on you. We love you Lord because you are our strength. You are our Rock, our fortress and our Saviour in whom we find protection. Lord, we ask for discipline over our emotions so they won't keep us in bondage. We thank you in advance for being our shield, the power who saves us, and our place of safety. We declare that in you, we will no longer be distressed because you are our Rock, our fortress, and our Deliverer! We shall be saved from mental and emotional distress because we know we have the victory in Jesus.

The battle is tough, but your Word states that all things work together for the good of those who love you, to those who are called according to your purpose. The adversary may think this warfare will keep us bound, but Lord, we believe in the power of your Word. We choose to walk in your power and your authority! Father, we can do all things through you who strengthens us—we can overcome distress through you! We understand this season of testing, but this testing that has overtaken us is common to everyone. You are faithful and will not let us be tested beyond our strength, but with the testing, you will also provide the way out so that we may be able to endure it! Precious Lord, please lead us to the way out, please guide us to the peace that our souls long for. Father, we thank you for healing and divine deliverance from being distressed. Amen.

Scriptural references: Psalm 46:1, 18:1-2; Proverbs 18:10; Nehemiah 8:10; 2 Samuel 22:2; Romans 8:28; Philippians 4:13

# Mental Health

PRAYER BY: VIDA WILLIAMS

Father God, you said if we call upon you, you would answer. I come to you for answers and deliverance. As we travel through life's rough highways and byways on this life journey, we face many challenges. We're forced to make difficult decisions. Sometimes it's hard to tell the left from the right, and right from wrong. Our decision-making process is challenged and we become confused. During these times, you told us to look to you because you would lead the way. We thank you because you're the source of our knowledge and strength. God, you provided us with the best and most reliable revenue –your Word. During times of distress, we can have an absence of judgment and discernment. God, it's in our weakness that we come to you for healing, for hope, and for our mental and spiritual well-being. We thank you because you're always here. With our faith, lead us and protect against dangers seen and unseen.

Lord, please give us the discernment and love to help others who might have lost their way in their thoughts. Show us how not to judge our fellow man. Show us how to use our Christian teachings and Bible studies to become more sensitive to others. Your Son Jesus showed total compassion by dying on the cross for us. We must follow His compassion and love for others. Amen.

# Churches

PRAYER BY: APOSTLE LYDIA WOODSON-SLOLEY

Father, we come before your throne of grace concerning your church, the church of Jesus Christ in the earth. LORD, we ask you to search the hearts of your ministers, every evangelist, every teacher, every preacher, every prophet, every apostle of the five-fold ministry, and all who sit in the congregation. LORD, we know that at the name of Jesus, every knee should bow, of things in heaven, and things on earth, and things under the earth. We ask for your continued grace and mercy upon our lives as we surrender our wills to walk uprightly before you.

LORD, stir up a "holy alertness" in your church during these troubled times. Let those who speak your gospel live by what they say they believe. Let them be examples not only in the pulpit, but in their homes when no one is watching. LORD, as you shake the nations, raise up your holy nation—the church—by the leading of your Holy Spirit into your path of righteousness during these end times. LORD, only you can separate the sheep from the goats, and the wheat from the tares. Raise up the righteous remnant who continue to lift up the bloodstained banner and walk in your mighty power in JESUS' matchless name. Amen.

Scriptural references: Acts 20:28; Philippians 2:10

# Resentment

PRAYER BY: NINA D. BROWN

Lord, we asked for your vindication, did you not hear our cries? As anger and revenge have become our new vindicators, protecting our hearts while slaughtering all who come too close. Yet everyday forms discomfort as it justified our quest to align with our protectors' bitterness and resentment.

We decided to wait became cause and effect was our promise it would never happen again. Protecting our space was our sole purpose to ensure victory. Yet heartbreak and despair have taken over as we were losing our strength to fight, so once more we cry for the comfort we once had.

O Lord, teach us to understand why we lost our peace; defend and deliver us from this affliction upon us. Grant us another chance to escape this slaughter of our souls. Deliver us from this affliction that continues to consume our souls and kill our spirits back to the untruth from whence it came.

Forgive us of our iniquities and direct our footsteps to forgive our enemies. Please turn this affliction to affirmation and this pain into purpose. This discomfort and pain desires to win our souls but we surrender what was given to us back to you. Our Rock and our shield, you allow us another opportunity to bow at your feet and surrender it all to you. Our affliction was meant to destroy us. Bring us back to you broken –but not destroyed. Revive us once again. Revive us, O Lord. Amen.

Scriptural reference: Ephesians 4:31-32

# Prayer for Men

PRAYER BY: BILLIE OGLESBY

Father in the name of Jesus, thank you for the spirit of the courageous conqueror of childhood sexual abuse. Despite the deep-rooted that she has endured, she is still standing. I speak to every place in her life that has been violated. Father, I pray against perpetual feelings of guilt, shame and self-blame. I bind those feelings right now in the matchless name of Jesus. I loose a newfound sense of peace, freedom, wholeness, and fearlessness.

The question of "Why?" will no longer torment her mind. I decree that she will step into the place of wholeness. I declare that even past abuse will work for her good and for your glory in Jesus' mighty name! The heaviness of the secret is no more. Even in this trauma, God, you will make good on your promise of healing. I'm expecting it and so it is! Depression and sadness shall be no more. I decree and declare that she will not make an excuse to be bitter and sabotage her blessings. Father God, do not allow her past to haunt her because she is free in the mighty name of Jesus. You are Jehovah-Rophe, the God who heals, and we believe this to be so!

Father God, may you heal this conqueror so that she becomes an ambassador of change, courage, and hope for others who experienced physical, mental, and emotional scars of childhood sexual abuse. In due season, may she be led to testify of her healing and deliverance! May conquerors arise in every nation to expose childhood sexual abuse and bring forth justice. We are change agents designed to shift the paradigm from brokenness to wholeness in Jesus' mighty name.

Sexual abuse is an attack of the enemy designed to steal our birth identities and create social ills such as teen pregnancy, addictions, and sexual promiscuity. You created us to prosper and be in good health, even as our souls prosper. May mental and emotional healing be this conqueror's portion. May she rise from the ashes of her past and walk boldly into her destiny as a new creation in Christ. Allow her life to be a picture of beauty and holiness. Send perverted thoughts of her self-worth into the abyss, never to return. Teach her to love and trust. May she also forgive her predator and others responsible for her pain in Jesus' mighty name we pray. Amen.

Scriptural references: Isaiah 61:1-3; Romans 8:28; Jeremiah 29:11; 3 John 1:2

# Belief

PRAYER BY: PATRICIA ETHEAH

Father, in the beginning you created man with leadership abilities and determination to procreate. They face the challenges of life and find ways to be providers for their families as well as for themselves. In Jesus' name, you put them in position and entrusted them with the glorious calling to protect and cherish their families. Give them an understanding and appreciation for the work that they're called to do, and for the many hats that they're called to wear. Lord, give them the ability to ward off the cares of this world that interfere with your plan and purpose chosen for them. They know that life is an amazing gift appropriated to give strength to families.

In the authority of the Lord Jesus Christ, we speak against the strongman fighting with men and their families. We cast away the spirit of poverty, lack, greed, selfishness, passivity, and procrastination over all men in Jesus' name. No weapon formed against their calling shall prosper. They are mighty men of riches, honor, wisdom, strength, and have God's blessings overtaking them. We declare that the Holy Spirit of joy, peace and love be poured out upon all men. Lord, strengthen their inner man and restore all things that have been stolen from them in Jesus' name.

Father you will always be first in their lives as they work as the spiritual covering for their families. As men of God, they will live according to your word and serve you daily, fulfilling the abundant life for their families in kindness and love. Your word says that a man is blessed when they fear you and delight greatly in your commandments. Help them remain faithful in prayer. Even when difficulties arise, they look to the Author and Finisher of their faith. Lord, they agree with you; they believe your word and wait patiently for your direction. When men delight in you, their descendants will rise up and be called blessed. Wealth and riches are in their homes in Jesus' name. They will provide guidance to other men and take their rightful place in this world for generations to come. In Jesus' name, amen.

Scriptural reference: Psalm 112:1

# Lying

PRAYER BY: GLORIA FONDJO

Dear Father, we apologize for all the times we forsook your name. We told lies so many times that it became normal to us. We failed to remember that by doing so, we disrespect you. Father, help us to accept the truth and tell the truth all the time. As our minds are wired to please others, sometimes even lying to do it, help us remember that we have nothing to prove to this world. You're the only one we want to please. Let the Holy Spirit be in our minds and hearts at all times to remind us to stay true to who we are. Help us remember never to change ourselves to adjust to this world's dimensions. Help us remember that if we lie, we hurt you and we hurt those we love.

Lord, we come before you and ask you to help us be better representatives of your Kingdom on earth. May we take pride in telling the truth, no matter how raw it is. May we favor true values and never be ashamed of our mistakes. Father, as your servants, we ask you to help our hearts be pure to accept the truth from others too. Without judging or criticizing, may we learn how to respect those who say the truth, even when they might have reasons not to. Abba, Father, we thank you for inspiring us every day to create graceful Christian lives from the truth of your Word, and most importantly, from the truth in our hearts. In Jesus' name, amen.

Scriptural reference: Proverbs 12:22

# Appreciation
PRAYER BY: ANTIONETTE LESLIE-HOLLAND

Most gracious Father in heaven, I just want to thank you for what you have done in our lives. If it hadn't been for you, your mercy and your grace, where would we be? We are grateful and thankful for our health and strength. We thank you for many blessings known and blessings to come. You shower blessings on us every day. Father God, you have no respect of persons because you love us all. We thank you for the provision of shelter, food, and clothing. We own nothing in this world so everything is provided by you. Lord, you told us to ask and it shall be given. We know we may not always receive the desires of our hearts, but we trust you to you know what's best for us. We know your answers could be yes or no, and sometimes you answer quickly or slowly. Lord, teach us how to be patient and to learn how to wait. Let us receive your answers without being angry or upset.

Lord, we thank you for every day of life. This is a blessing all by itself. We are thankful for knowing you as our Lord and Savior. So many have left this earth not knowing you, but we are grateful for what you have done. You love this entire world so that you gave your only begotten Son to die for us. He died on Calvary's cross so that we can have eternal life in heaven. Father God, you sent your Son Jesus to die for the sins of this world. He was wounded for our transgressions and bruised for our iniquities. He paid a debt He did not owe. We're forever thankful and grateful for what you have done in our lives. You did it all for us and if we receive your Son Jesus as our Lord and Savior, we are saved by your grace. Father, thank you for the gift of the Holy

Spirit who teaches us and guides us every day. Thank you for the Word and your instructions that teach us how to live in this world until you return. I pray this in the name of the Father, and the Son, and the precious Holy Spirit. Amen.

Scriptural reference: Psalm 24:1

# Police

PRAYER BY: MINISTER TYRA FRAZIER

Heavenly Father, I approach your throne of grace as humbly as I know how. I come reverencing your holy and righteous name. I come with my brothers and sisters touching and agreeing that your will shall be done in the lives of your people. That the blood of Jesus that covers us from day to day is still working some two-thousand years later. Lord, we come on behalf of every police officer in the land. We come asking for a special covering over their lives. We come, O God, praying for the blood of Jesus to cover and keep them. We come, O God, asking you to protect them from the cares of this world and from those who intentionally choose to do evil unto them. Lord, we pray daily for them to return home to their loved ones. We pray daily for their willingness to serve in a time like this. We pray daily that the life of every police officer matters –at work, at home, and in the Kingdom. God, we thank you for their protection through the land and for their willingness to say yes.

Lord, we pray for their strength. We pray for their understanding of the power they have so they would not misuse it. We pray for their wisdom to handle the population at large with care. We pray for their changed hearts so they will not view all citizens as being the same. God, we pray for a change in relationship between officers and the community they serve. We need healing and a reprieve from all injustices that were done. We are in such a hard place right now God, but I am convinced that you will pull us through. Our hearts and minds have been cleared to focus on you, God. As police officers protect and serve, remove all the dead areas in their lives. Mend broken spirits and remove danger so they can do their jobs effectively. In the name of Jesus, I pray. Amen.

# Death

PRAYER BY: MOZELLEN DOBIE

Jesus! Jesus! Jesus! I humbly come to you, Jesus. Father, you know the hearts of your people and you are touched with our feelings. Father I pray that you give the comfort that only you can. Hallelujah! There is trouble in the land but God, you're in the plan. Hallelujah! You promised that you prepared a place for us. Death is not the end. This earth is not our home. Help Jesus, when hearts are over whelmed. Help us to go to that secret place in you and find comfort. Give us the peace that passes all understanding. Jesus! Jesus! Jesus! There is something about your name, Jesus! It is strong and powerful. Father, as I pray for the over whelming deaths happening, I ask that you help your people hold on to your word. Help us know how your ways are not our ways, neither are your thoughts like ours. You are the wise and all-knowing Savior. Jesus, you make no mistakes. I pray for heavy hearts that are crying. I speak peace. Weeping may endure for a night, but you promised that joy comes in the morning.

Help Lord! Help Lord! Help Lord! Jesus, your people are crying out and you promised that you would answer them and that right early. I pray in your name because your name saves, it heals, and it delivers. Help them get through time even if they don't understand it. Jesus, help them to continue giving you the glory, even in death. I pray that nothing will separate them from the love of God, not even death.

Help Lord! Help Lord! Help Lord! Jesus help! Jehovah shalom, you are peace. Jesus, I pray that their souls die in you. I pray that they received you as their Lord and Savior. Your word declares that we must be born again of the water and the Spirit. We must be filled with the gift of the Holy Ghost. Jesus, all souls belong to you. You are the way, the truth, and the light. No man comes to the Father except through you. Jesus, I pray for the souls of your people. I pray that they hear you say "Well done!" in Jesus' name. Amen.

# First Responders

PRAYER BY: VERNETTA DRUMMOND-MERCER

Father God, we thank you for those who bravely risk their lives during this pandemic. As these first responders travel to and from work, we ask you to bless their homes and their whereabouts. God, we also ask you to bless their loved ones who may have pre-existing medical conditions. Even with them, O God, encourage them to be strong and courageous. Let them know that you will never leave them or forsake them. Let them know that you have covered them under your divine protection. Please' cover every first responder with your love and give them comfort to know that you are a real God who saves and heals. Even now, we pray that you increase their faith and that you open up their understanding concerning their purpose for such a time as this. God, grant them divine strategies in how to handle every emergency that comes their way. Show them how to trust you as they handle every situation with care. Help them to lean not to their own understanding and to allow you to direct their paths. After every shift, allow them to cast their cares upon you and to release what they can't control to you.

Give them creative ways on how to persevere in serving and protecting the lives they are entrusted over. God, let them know that in the midst of everything, no weapon formed against them shall prosper and their peace is guaranteed as long as they focus on you in all they do. Father, we bind panic and fatigue on their jobs and in their homes, and we loose your peace that surpasses all understanding. Lord, your promises are yes and amen. You said whatever we bind on earth shall be bound in heaven, and whatever we loose on earth shall be loosed in heaven. We rebuke the spirits of heaviness, oppression, and depression over their minds as they sleep at night, and we release the mind of Jesus Christ. For those first responders who are saved, let their light shine so that people who are suffering would know the love of Christ that shines so brightly through them. Help them understand that they are purposefully on assignment for your Kingdom. For first responders who are not saved, Father, we pray that they would give their hearts to you! In Jesus name, Amen.

Scriptural reference: Psalm 18:6

# Sex Trafficking

PRAYER BY: DR. LESLIE DUROSEAU

Early in the morning shall I rise and seek your face. As the Son shines down brightly upon His children, have your light to shine on us. Darkness cannot dim your light, for your light penetrates the darkness of this world.

Dear Lord, we are your most vulnerable victims of this dark world. Come and rescue us. Release us from this bondage. We praise you, great Jehovah, and we humble ourselves before you. You are the God of justice, of love, and of peace. You are the God who despises evil and wickedness. Release us from those who torture us.

We lament, we humble ourselves, we prostrate ourselves before the true and living God. The One who is the truth, the way, and the life. Daily do we cry out to you, Great Jehovah Rapha, and we wait on you to heal us. Daily do we cry out and we ask where is our God? Our God who is Emmanuel, our God who is with us and within us. May the pneuma of God cleanse us; wash us with hyssop and remove all inequity.

We shall rise up and be restored. We shall be redeemed by the blood of the Lamb. Hallelujah to the King of kings and Lord of lords. Great Jehovah Rapha, our healer, Great Jehovah-Nissi, our deliverer. Great Jehovah Shalom, the God who is our peace. We wait on you, for those who wait upon the Lord will have their strength be restored. And we will be renewed. Amen.

Scriptural reference: Isaiah 40:27-31

# Verbal Abuse

PRAYER BY: TENARIA DRUMMOND-SMITH

Hallelujah, thank you Lord, thank you JESUS. Lord, I ask that you would heal every broken heart that was told that they would never amount to anything and that no one would ever love or want them. O God, we know that you are the God of love. Hallelujah, thank you Lord, thank you for loving us even at times when we didn't love ourselves. I ask in the name of Jesus that you heal the hurt of everyone who has been called names. Lord, I pray that you would not allow them to receive that hurt in the name of Jesus. Lord, I ask in your name that they will not do the same to others as it was done unto them because words have power. We know how a person can believe what they hear if they keep hearing that they are nothing.

Lord, you tell us in your word to forgive them, for they know not what they do. O God, I ask and pray that whoever reads this would know that no weapon formed against them will prosper in the name of Jesus, and that every word spoken that was not of you will return back to where it came from. Lord, I ask right now that those who speak negative things to innocent people would be delivered from their anger caused by someone in their past who hurt them. Lord, we know that many things we do extend from things that were done to us. I pray that we will all be free of name-calling and speaking with harsh words in Jesus' name. Amen, and amen.

Scriptural reference: Isaiah 54:17

# Grief

PRAYER BY: SOPHIA L. GREENE

Heavenly Father, I come before you with a repentant spirit to acknowledge your holiness. As your daughter, I submit all hearts in mourning all over the world. Please visit all homes and hearts. Give us a place of comfort and peace as we mourn the losses we experienced in our time on this earth. I pray for healing of all who have lost family members and friends in this lifetime and have not grieved over them because the pain was too much to bear. I thank God that we have access to a burden carrier who is available to carry all our pain and worries.

God of the universe, as you walk through the world with your omnipresence, please touch hearts and have us recognize how your love and presence is the answer to all our situations. Show us how to keep our eyes and hearts on you so we can learn to love each other as you love us. Thank you, Abba.

# Dialysis

PRAYER BY: ROBERTA JONES-JOHNSON

Hallelujah! Father, I thank you for another day of life. I give you all the honor and I come praising your holy name. Father, you're the only One who deserves it because we come short of your glory.

In the name of Jesus, I come asking that your will be done for dialysis patients. If it be continued dialysis or kidney replacement, let it be so according to your will. Remove every impurity that causes their kidneys not to function correctly. Bless the hands of medical doctors, nurses, and technicians as they perform dialysis on their patients. As you perform your will, I pray that dialysis patients will have restored appetites and the energy needed to regain strength in their bodies.

Father, as only you can, I ask you to extend your mercy and grace toward them. We might ask why this is happening but you told us to trust you, the great God, with all our heart and lean not to our own understanding. You're the Great Doctor, and if it be your will, I ask you to reverse kidney failure in our loved ones. Father, heal their kidneys in the name of Jesus. As you created them to do, let them filter toxins and impurities out from our bodies.

You said you won't leave us nor forsake us, and I stand on your word. I ask you to give families strength to hold onto their faith with their loved ones being in this condition. Father, I pray for the coming of your Kingdom that will do away with all sickness and disease. I speak healing in the precious name of Jesus. Amen.

Scriptural references: Proverbs 3:5; Psalm 27:9; Hebrews 13:5

# Low Self-Esteem

PRAYER BY: PROPHETESS VON BRAND

Father, with our prayers we lift up those who battle with the spirit of low self-esteem. We come against every attack of insecurity and inferiority that the enemy tries to make them have against themselves. We break the back of Satan today and every day, and we remind your children of what your Word says concerning them being fearfully and wonderfully made. You tell them that they can do all things through you who gives them strength. You tell them that no weapon formed against them shall prosper, and they will refute every tongue that accuses them. The power of the tongue that lied and told them they were nobody or would ever amount to anything has already been defeated. It was defeated on the cross. Hallelujah, glory to God!

Your word reminds us that we could be healed, not just as a physical thing, but in our brokenness, our spiritual and our emotional states. We decree and declare ourselves free today. We celebrate our wholeness! We decree and declare that the flood gates of heaven are open on our behalf as we celebrate our victory today! Hallelujah, we rejoice today because we're free!

Scriptural references: Psalm 139:14; Philippians 4:13; Isaiah 54:17

# Witchcraft
PRAYER BY: ANNETTA DRUMMOND

Father, we praise you, we honor you, we give you all the glory. We thank you for the authority you have given unto us your children. Your Word declares that whatever we bind on earth is bound in heaven. Your word declares that we suffer not a witch to live. We command every witch, warlock, soothsayer, astrologer, necromancer, obeah and tarot card reader to repent or die by fire in Jesus' name.

I bind every negative and ungodly word spoken against our lives. I break and utterly destroy every spirit of confusion, torment, fear, control and manipulation in the name of Jesus.

I break and destroy the power of witchcraft, deception, seduction sorcery, and every intimidation directed to me and my family in Jesus' name.

I decree freedom from every dark power, every astral projection, every Jezebelic spirit, false prophetic words, controllers, manipulators, sorcerers, counterfeits, soul ties, lying spirits, lying dreams, and lying visions. Incubus and Succubus spirits, I declare you null and void in all your activities in Jesus' name.

Every evil word spoken over our lives by those in authority, I declare it null and void in the name of Jesus. It will not manifest in our lives. I command that every curse from both sides of my family be broken and no longer in effect in my bloodline in Jesus' name.

I break and destroy every spirit of rejection and abandonment, and I replace you by the spirit of acceptance and loyalty in Jesus name. Everywhere our names are being spoken for evil; I command that they catch fire in the name of Jesus. I break and destroy every spirit of conspiracy against me and my family. I release confusion into the camp of the enemy to fight against themselves and totally annihilate themselves.

Now Father, remove every residue of evil-spoken words, curses and hexes from our lives by the blood of Jesus. We repent of every sin known and unknown that has opened the door to any attacks upon us in Jesus name. Lord, your word declares that if we confess our sins, you are faithful and just to forgive us for our sins. We dedicate our lives to the will of Christ and Christ alone. We submit ourselves to Jesus Christ and to His word in Jesus' name. Amen.

Scriptural reference: Exodus 2:18

# United Nations

PRAYER BY: QUEEN MOTHER

O God of the universe, we come to you this perfect day in your divine grace that protects us in your world. We bow down before you and worship you. We ask you, our Creator and giver of all life, to bless the United Nations. In their deliberations as Member States, we ask that you be a part of their discussion for creating a better world that we could pass on to our children. O God, we stretch our arms out to you as we look toward the hills where our help comes from, to embrace us, to love us and nourish us every day of our lives. We ask you to divinely guide and counsel us. Help us live in your presence. We came here with nothing, and we will leave here with nothing. Help us find comfort of peace and tranquility with each other as we live with one another.

This is our prayer that we echo to you this day. Teach us humility, teach us wisdom, teach us understanding, and above all, teach us how to care for each other. We ask that you never leave us or forsake us. We ask for your healing grace in the world, from the north to the south, from the east to the west. Teach us how to be good stewards in protecting every dominion of your world. We acknowledge you O God; we know that you run the world and we run around in the world. We want to thank you for allowing us to do so. So be it. Amen.

# Divorce

PRAYER BY: JANET LENNOX

Abba Father, we thank you for who are and who you will become. We give you praise, honor and glory. You are God of creation, the Father of Abraham, Isaac and Jacob, and we come to you only in the name of Jesus. We ask you for forgiveness of sins known and unknown. We repent of our past sins of fornication, unfaithfulness, rejection and betrayal of our spouses. Lord God, you have ordained marriage but because our hearts were hardened against one another, the spirit of divorce crept in. Lord God, we come against the spirit of divorce attacking the lives of your people. Your word says that Moses permitted divorce because our hearts were hardened, but it was not this way from the beginning. Give us clean hearts and a contrite spirit towards our spouses.

We command ordination of marriage to come back into alignment right now in Jesus' name. We command every curse of divorce sent by the enemy to be scattered by fire right now. Every divorce altar that has our names on it, we command them to catch fire now in Jesus' name. Lord God, we terminate every spirit of confusion hiding in and attacking our minds. Let every enemy that is camouflaging in our relationships be exposed by the fire of God right now. You said that Satan comes to steal, destroy and kill, but you came to give life and you give it more abundantly. We speak abundant life into our marriages. We bind and cast out the spirit of divorce right now in the name of Jesus. We speak wholeness of the minds, bodies and souls of those who plan to divorce. We decree and declare that they shall not divorce, but cleave as one flesh as God has spoken from the beginning in Jesus' name. Thank you, Jesus, for recovery and healing of our marriages in Jesus' name. Amen!

Scriptural reference: Matthew 19:8

# Teen Mothers

PRAYER BY: DAWN GRANTHAM

O Lord, I'm standing in gap and praying for teenage mothers. This is a reality of our lives and it's a huge responsibility. Some have given up on their education and dropped out of school. They found it difficult to retain their lessons while trying to care for their children. Bless them to continue with their education so they can be productive citizens and avoid living as statistics in poverty. Bless them financially. Give them wisdom and equip them to become entrepreneurs and business leaders. Bless them with high paying jobs with benefits and retirement pensions. O Lord, I pray that you open up doors of opportunity for them so that they lack nothing, want for nothing, and have need for nothing. Bless their families to support and encourage them, and not shame them. Bring forth good mentors and role models who used to be where they are. People expect young mothers to become perfect mothers immediately. How quickly do we forget that these are babies raising babies while facing new challenges of motherhood?

O Lord, remind them that they can do all things through Christ. Help them strive and do their best in this new chapter of life. Where they're weak, help them to be strong. Give them strength, courage, and the will of God to love and care for their babies unconditionally and with integrity. When fear and doubt creep in, show them that they can get through by the grace of God. Provide them with guidance and prepare them emotionally. Build up their self-esteem as they face criticism from their peers. Help them manage and prioritize their time so they won't feel overwhelmed and consumed by their tasks. Help them remember to love themselves and take care of themselves. If they do this, they can continually love their babies. Put in their hearts and minds that being young mothers shall not deviate them from God's purpose. In spite of their circumstances, instill in them just how wonderful they are. Amen.

Scriptural references: Titus 2:11; Psalm 139:14

# Domestic Violence

PRAYER BY: MIRANDA RIVERS

O Lord, hear their cries of those in domestic violence situations. There are so many who are suffering in silence. Lord, I ask you deliver them to a safe place so they can begin to heal. Surround them with your angels in Jesus name.

Father God, I ask you to help children to feel loved and cared for in the midst of these situations. May they find comfort in knowing that you are the Deliverer of their freedom and peace. Faithful God, please heal and restore their belief in you. Help them trust and open up their hearts to love. Surround them with your angels in Jesus' name.

We pray for the hearts of the abusers. Lord, touch the hearts of those who hurt their loved ones. Heal their hearts and guide their thinking so that they may seek your ways. Help them know that everyone should be loved, honored, and respected. Faithful God, we also ask that you help them to acknowledge how they are harming others so that they can learn to despise their own behavior and come to a true repentance.

Precious Lord, You constructed us in your likeness and breathed life into us, a life you want us to live abundantly. We ask you to surround them with your safekeeping and shelter them with your love. Allow them to enjoy good health, healing, strength, and peace. We pray they will feel and know your presence to seek a way out. We ask all these things in Jesus name. Amen!

Scriptural references: Psalm 107:20, 27:10

# Wisdom
PRAYER BY: SARAH NICHOLS

Heavenly Father, you're our God and holy name. Every good and perfect gift comes from you. We thank you for your word that brings wisdom. We pray for light in our understanding of your word so that we may walk in wisdom and impart it in everything we do. What a privilege and as honor it is to be called one of your own. We're wonderfully and fearfully made. Made in your image and likeness, we're loved with an everlasting love and we're grateful. Father, we thank you for giving us wisdom through your word, and for the knowledge and understanding that comes from it. You said if we lack wisdom, we can ask for it and you'll give it to us generously without finding fault in us for not knowing how to handle situations. Help us live our lives with wisdom so that we may cherish understanding and prosper from it.

Father, thank you for all the blessing you've given us in finding your wisdom. It was only by your Holy Spirit that we found wisdom and understanding. Your word tells us how finding wisdom is worth far more and is more profitable than silver and gold. It's more precious than rubies and nothing that we know can compare to it. By wisdom, you'll give us blessings of long life, riches, honor, and peace. Lord, we thank you for giving us the desire to seek wisdom and gain understanding for your glory. We thank you for the mistakes we made before we knew wisdom. We thank you because you forgave our mistakes and helped us move on with the assurance that our latter will be greater than our former. We thank you because our past isn't held against us. We're able to move on because you gave us a new start. God, as you blessed Solomon with wisdom to be a blessing to your people, make us vessels of wisdom to help all who we meet. Guide us with your wisdom so that we may say the right things to those in need. We give you glory and honor, for it is so and it's already done. In Jesus' name, amen.

# Unity

PRAYER BY: CAMEO BOONE

Father in Heaven, I thank you. Thank you for your love, your mercy, and your grace. Father, thank you for your faithfulness, and for your endurance, Hallelujah! Lord, thank you for being long-suffering with us. Thank you for all that you do for us on a daily basis, Elohim. Holy Spirit, fill us up and allow your Spirit to speak to our spirit, for the Spirit searches all things of God. Thank you, Father, because you know all the desires of our hearts and you grant them according to your will. You told us to come boldly to the throne of grace, that we may have mercy and find grace to help in time of need.

We need your help, dear God, with unity! Grant us a spirit of unity amongst people, Elohim. We have been divided and deceived for so long. It's s not by chance because we know that satan is the author of confusion and division. We also know that he has power but no authority! The children of Elohim have power AND authority through our savior, Jesus Christ, and the Holy Spirit! We must be unified as one people under one body of Christ. At the tower of Babel, you said we were all one people, so there aren't any races, just human beings. There wasn't supposed to be religions, we're supposed to be followers of Jesus, therefore help us shed these denominations dear Father! They're a tool for the enemy to divide the children of God.

Help us be unified in the family for our survival. Help us be unified amongst spiritual leadership through corporate prayer, because we wrestle not with flesh and blood but against principalities, against powers, against the rulers of darkness.

Jesus, help us be unified in love, unified in faith, unified in mind set, and most of all, unified in CHRIST! Let the women of this prayer journal be examples of how unity can knock down the strongholds of this nation, for we know that with unified prayer, one can chase a thousand, and two can put ten-thousand to flight. Amen!

Scriptural references: 1 Corinthians 2:10; Hebrews 4:16; Ephesians 6:12; Deuteronomy 32:30

# Willpower

PRAYER BY: CYRINTHIA HILL-FLOWERS

Father in the name of Jesus, I pray for those who lack the will power to go forth and do what you are calling them to do. I pray for those who have a divine purpose but are fearful and hold back because they lack willpower. I pray for those who won't move forward because they are fearful and feel that they will fail. God, let them know that there is no failure in you. You have given them power over all power of the enemy, and power to accomplish your will in their lives. The dreams and visions they have shall be done in your name. Nothing by any means shall hinder, block or stop them. I bind the enemy who comes to steal, kill and destroy. In the name of Jesus, I speak strength to stand in the presence of God to fulfill their calling.

Many are called Lord, but few are chosen. Let your chosen vessels seek the willpower and anointing to GO! God, they will be empowered to do your will. God, you are the one who has gifted them. They can't hide their talents. They shall do what you have spoken over their lives. Some hold the keys to somebody else's deliverance. Some have ministries to bring forth or pull out of others. They must come forth in Jesus' name. They will succeed, and not quit or give in. Thy will be done over the lives of your people in Jesus' name! The conquerors must come forward and the visionaries must come forward. No one's dream shall die because of the lack of willpower. It is God who gives courage in Jesus' name. Amen!

Scriptural references: Luke 10:19; Psalm 34:4, 23:4, 27:1, 16:11; John 10:10; Matthew 22:14, 25:14-30; Ephesians 4:8; Joshua 1:7-9; Romans 8:37

# Family Dysfunction

PRAYER BY: JOYCE ROLLINS

God, I pray that you go into the midst of families across the world and set order. Father, send forth your Spirit who makes loving and understanding easy. Lord, your word says that we should rend our hearts and not our garments. We should return to you, our God, because you're gracious and compassionate, slow to anger, abounding in love and relenting from sending calamity. God, show us your compassion and love. Protect families from calamity. Bind them together in love and perfect unity with cords that cannot be broken. Cause the rivalry to dismantle at the root. Send peace to the homes of broken families. God, I speak to ancestral curses, generational assignments, and remnants of sins of the forefathers. I take control of the lingering spirit that causes pain and dysfunction. I command you to leave; you can no longer live here. I cast you back to the pit of hell in the name of Jesus Christ the risen Savior. I destroy every plan, every event, every assignment, every attachment, every execution, every death, and every separation in the name of Jesus. I speak total healing, and healthy reconnection.

From family heads down to the children, God, be a present help for them. They will walk together in love and protect one another. They're healthy families in the name of Jesus. God, send husbands the ability to lead families; Give them the heart and compassion to love their wives and children. Give them examples who will show them how to function in your word. God, show wives how to love their husbands and be strong for them to make it through storms. Give wives the fortitude to follow your word concerning their position in family. Show them how to allow husbands to be head and protector of the family and the home. Father, I pray that you pour stability over families across the world. Cover them for generations to come. I proclaim that there will be no lack, and all their needs will be met. I proclaim that the joy of the Lord will meet them each day. Father, I declare unity in our families. I'm thanking you in advance. Let your will be done in Jesus' name. Amen.

Scriptural references: Joel 2:13; Colossians 3:14

# Peace

PRAYER BY: CHERYLN OLIVER-McKAY

Dear Lord, as your meek and humble servant, I come before you. We just want to thank you Lord God, just for waking us up, for bringing us through another night and leading us into this day. Father, I pray this prayer of peace for everyone. Lord God, I'm praying for the peace that surpasses all understanding. Our lives with are filled with so many distractions and situations that keep us bound and confused. We get bound by our own thinking, worrying, and trying to understand things that we can't possibly understand without you. Your thoughts are not ours, and our thoughts are not yours. Your people are looking for answers in the world where there are none, and for doing this, your people have become overwhelmed, stressed, and depressed. The enemy is clogging our minds with all manner of evil that keeps us from hearing from you. Lord, I ask you to help us remember that although there will be many trials that we have to face in this life, we should hold on to you. We should keep our minds on you by staying in your word so your word can be alive in us.

Lord God, I pray that your people reach out for you and receive the peace that will surpass their understanding. In your word, we trust you for that peace, and I know it will bring spiritual insight and understanding to those who will receive you. Father, have mercy on us right now, for you tell us to cast our cares upon you because you care for us. You tell us that your peace shall keep our hearts and minds through Christ Jesus. You tell us to be careful about nothing, but in everything by prayer and supplication with thanksgiving, to let our requests be made known to you. Lord, my request is for peace for everyone all around the world in Jesus' name I pray, amen.

Scriptural references: 1 Peter 5:7; Philippians 4:6-7

# For the Nation

PRAYER BY: ESTHER BURGESS

O Lord, righteous and holy Redeemer, God of mercy and judgement. Glory, honor, adoration, and power belong to you. A scepter of righteousness, we honor your holy name. Heavenly Father, I come before you in the matchless name of our Lord and savior Jesus Christ, interceding for this nation. Lord, our forefathers have sinned and we continue to commit iniquity. We have left our first love and gone astray, each to our own way. We have rebelled against thy precepts, and with the choices we've made, we have brought judgement upon ourselves. Our land is defiled, we are in a backsliding state, and our children are walking in disobedience, from being raised without the fear of God. We have compromised the words of the living God and accepted false teachings. We are covenant breakers, rebellious, full of envy, unrighteous, backbiters, and disobedient. Yes, we have sinned against thee and done evil in thy sight. Lord, the curse of sin is poured out upon this nation because we have not obeyed thy voice.

Merciful Father we need you, we can't do it on our own. Give us a heart of repentance. Help us turn from our wicked ways and turn to you with our whole heart, so that your countenance may shine upon us and heal us. We have tried to operate independently from you, but Lord, we have failed time after time, and time again. O Lord hear us, O Lord heal us, O Lord restore us, I beseech you. Look at the desolation of this nation and have mercy. Lord, withhold thy wrath from us for thy mercy's sake, because who can stand in thy judgement, or who can pardon us but you? Father, I pray that your mercy and grace continue to abide with us, for if you should withdraw yourself, whither shall we go? Lord, we are broken. Only you and you alone can heal us, for our soul is destitute without you. All nations are as grass before you and are counted for nothing. You alone can restore, and you alone can redeem. My God, incline thine ear, and hear. Open thine eyes and behold the desolation of the people thou hast created. As we present our supplications before you, hear and answer. I pray in Jesus' matchless and wonderful name. Amen.

# Teachers

PRAYER BY: THERESA BYRD

Our Father who art in heaven, I'm calling on your holy name with my head bowed down, my eyes closed, and with a crying heart. So many of your children nowadays are attempting suicide as their way out. When I hear the word, it sends chills up and down my spine. It's a scary situation to even think about. LORD, please touch their minds and hearts today. Cover them with your blood in their going out, their coming in, in their laying down as well as their rising up.

This is a vicious cycle taking place all around the world. LORD, I know that you're the only one who can stop this madness. All of them have different reasons, but the load must be too heavy for any of them to bear. You are an awesome God who knows all things. I'm praying for them and hoping that you send the Comforter their way. They're in need of being saved. LORD, strengthen them; show them the way. Please lift them up for your glory. Amen.

Scriptural reference: Psalm 61:1-2

# Debt

PRAYER BY: PASTOR SHAWN QUALLO

Father in the name of Jesus, we come binding the spirit of poverty away from your people. We destroy the spirit of debt; we bind up mismanagement of money that opens the door to debt. We sever this stronghold off our lives and the lives of our children. We destroy the spirit of debt and we break the spirit of distress that binds your people's lives. Lord, we thank you for causing debt to flee in Jesus' name. Anything that cause our money to scatter, we reverse those curses now. We call wealth to be attracted to us in the name of Jesus. Lord, we thank you for opening the doors to wealth and overflow of our finances. Lord, you delivereth the poor in his affliction, and you openeth their ears in oppression. Open our eyes to see and discern that seducing spirit of creditors. We bind their tricks to control us; we destroy this stronghold now in Jesus' name. We thank you for hearing our cries. Oppressive systems will be broken and will release us from the spirit of lack.

We pray now that the doors of employment be open for those seeking jobs in Jesus' name. Lord, cause your divine favor to open doors that no man can shut, and shut doors that no man can open. Those needing increase on their jobs, we call forth divine promotion that will destroy poverty. Those with business ideas, we call them forth just like you asked Moses to show you what you put in his hand. We decree that we are equipped to destroy the spirit of debt and financial bondage. Lord, we call forth the supernatural awakening. We call forth your people to gather vessels to collect, to multiply resources and build wealth, just like your prophet Elisha told the woman to borrow pots and gather the oil. We thank you for the wealth that will manifest with us as it did for that woman with the oil. We will not die because of financial distress. We thank you for giving us all things concerning life, and we thank you for breaking our debt. That debt is broken for us to leave an inheritance to our children's children. We thank you for the wealth of the sinner that is stored up for the righteous in Jesus' name. Amen.

Scriptural references: 2 Kings 4:1-7; Job 36:15; Proverbs 13:22

# Healing

PRAYER BY: JACQUELENE SCRUGGS

Our heavenly Father, we come before you thanking you for everything. We thank you for waking us up this morning being in our right minds, with blood running warm in our veins, and for the activities of our limbs. Thank you Jesus, hallelujah, hallelujah, glory to your name. We thank you for our life, our health and strength. Jesus, you are so wonderful to us. We give you all the glory and the praise. We thank you for the gift of life. Lord, we thank you for healing from the crown of our heads to the soles of our feet. Lord, we thank you for all things great and small. We know all our help comes from the Lord. We thank you, Jesus, for being our all-seeing eyes. Lord, we ask you to remember the sick and shut-in, and to heal them.

Remember the ones in the nursing homes and in the hospitals. Lord, give them health in our minds and bodies so those who suffer may overcome sickness and have the victory in Jesus' mighty name. We thank you Jesus, glory hallelujah, glory to your name. Lord, we ask you to comfort the sick and the suffering. The woman at the well touched the hem of your garment and received your healing. You gave her faith to walk in victory and freedom. God, we trust you to heal every form of sickness in our bodies. Jesus, heal us and save our souls. God, you are the only one who can restore our health. You are the only one who has the power to comfort us and give us hope to believe that you can do all things. Lord, you are the healer of our souls. You are so faithful to us. Jesus, we thank you for being there in the time of our need. You are so worthy. You are our way-maker. Lord, heal us from all our infirmities. We believe all things are possible. We thank you, Jesus, because prayer transcends all things. We thank you for your goodness. Lord, we declare victory in your name. Jesus, we thank you. Amen.

Scriptural references: James 5:14-15; Isaiah 53:5

# Pornography
PRAYER BY: WENDYANN WILLIAMS

Lord, I lift up the men who have a personal relationship with you and whose heart's desire is to get to know you on a deeper level. Please allow them to have the mind of Christ so they'll think like you and honor you by putting you first in their lives. Help them to always remember to wear the helmet of salvation so they can make wise decisions to guard against the negative thoughts of the enemy. Allow them to see with spiritual eyes that the battles they face are not against flesh and blood. Their battles against their past, their weaknesses, their shortcomings and insecurities. Let them see how the enemy uses these things against them so they may always wear the full armor of God to withstand the attacks of his enemy.

Help them keep their eyes focused on you so they will know how to turn away from temptation and seek you for deliverance. Protect their ears in what they hear so they'll only hear from you and know your small still voice in the midst of all noise and confusion. Help them choose their words wisely so they'll be pleasing to you. Lord, may their speech always be free from perversion and be uplifting, gracious, and astute, so that others may want to get to know you. Protect their hearts from evil desires and deception and show them how to look to you as the source of direction and strength.

Guide their footsteps wherever they go so that they'll be pleasing to you. Show them how to walk humbly in your grace and with godly countenance so your character may be an example to others. Most of all, show them and help them know how much you love them. I pray this prayer in Christ's name, amen.

Scriptural references: Ephesians 6:10-17; Colossians 4:6; Psalm 19:14

# Nurses

PRAYER BY: SHERRELL D. MIMS

Jesus Christ, divine Healer of all who blessed our ancestors in faith, bless, heal, and restore ones who are sick right now. May the God of our souls send an overflow of healing and compassion to expedite healing. We humble ourselves at your throne of grace. We ask that your divine hand inspire, touch, and supply thy wisdom in every situation. Bless everyone we come in contact who might be damaged, traumatized, or just downright sick.

Jesus, let your help not be far away. We pray for complete healing and restoration of the afflicted, from the crown of their heads to the soles of their feet. Let there be healing for the souls and bodies of your children right now Jesus, for with you, all things are possible. We cannot do anything without your love and guidance. Jesus, as we come near the sick, show us how to have a compassionate touch and kind words to speak into their lives. Show us how to take care of them as if we were taking care of you.

Jesus, when you ascended into heaven, you left the care of the sick to those in the profession of nursing. Let us have no purpose other than to glorify our Father in heaven to sustain the life of His children around the world. Jesus, let us dedicate our lives to the care of your children today. I thank you for choosing us to shine your light through the darkness of illness. When we finish working all through the day or the night, let us sleep in peace, knowing that we've done all we could do for your children here on earth. And if we helped just one, then we truly did it to serve you. Jesus, you send us as angels into the sick room. May we always be what you called us to be. Hallelujah! Amen, and so be it!

# Elderly

PRAYER BY: D.D. HOUSTON DUPREE

Heavenly Father, I thank you for our elders. I think of their place in our society today and I pray that they receive the assistance they need during these trying times. I pray that our society recognizes the value of our elderly. I pray that people will reflect on the importance of the family unit and the values that our elderly give the family. I pray our society realizes how helpful our elders are to us. I pray that our youth will reevaluate their viewpoint of our elderly and try to learn a thing or two from them. Lord, I pray that our youth would be thankful and never cast away or forsake our elders when they're weak.

Dear Lord, bless our people with hearts that care for people of all ages. Continue to give us wisdom and capability to help our elders because they've given so much to us. Lord, we thank you for our elders who blessed us with their time and knowledge, their spiritual and emotional support, their encouragement, love, respect, friendship, confidence, and their personal stories. They showed us their perseverance, their devotion, and they shared their faith with us about you being our Heavenly Father. Amen.

# Grandparents

PRAYER BY: JEAN THOMPSON

King of kings and Lord of lords, I thank you for being mighty and awesome. You've blessed not only me and my family, but the whole world knows your mercy and kindness. With our grandchildren, you've allowed us to see another generation come forth as a blessing and a precious gift from God. Jesus, you blessed us to be grandparents by giving us long life and abundance. You've shown us how we must give love and guidance, but we also have to discipline and protect with God's strength and power. I pray that the Holy Spirit dwells richly inside of grandparents daily. I pray that we continue to hold true to all your promises of seeing generations to come.

You promised that all things work together for our good. Jehovah, please bless grandparents with wisdom, knowledge, self-control, and the commitment to be a blessing to our grandchildren. Help us share our experiences with them and open up the way to make it easier for them to travel. Help us be beacons of light as elders for a generation of children losing their way. I pray in the mighty and merciful name of Jesus Christ that our youth can live to see their children's children. God, all the glory goes to you for what you've done and will do. We can't do this walk alone. Lord, we need you to hold our hand. Walk with us, talk with us, and guide us. Thank you, Lord. Amen.

Scriptural references: Genesis 48:9; Psalm 37:25, 90:12, 103:17; Proverbs 16:1; Isaiah 40:28-31; 2 Timothy 1:5

# Joy

PRAYER BY: LESLEY GEORGE

Father, I thank you for the joy we feel in knowing that we're specially made in your eyes. You created us with purpose. You gave us joy as our internal regulator. That joy pushes us on days where we feel insecure, unloved, or unworthy. The joy you gave us inspires us to keep that flame burning on the inside of us, no matter what's happening on the outside. The presence of joy shows up even in the midst of this COVID-19 pandemic. You still wake us up daily and with a smile.

We have joy knowing that we serve a Mighty God! We might be challenged in our daily lives, but in our souls, we know our joy won't disappear. We experience joy less on some days than on other days, so Lord, we ask you for the strength to hold on to our joy. Our joy regulates our hope. It fills in the crevasse of despair when life doesn't meet our expectations. Father, help us stay full of joy. Help us keep our cup filled with love and hope, and help us recognize people you placed in our lives to remind us of your joy when we're feeling down. Help us to remember that your joy means hope. Amen.

# Military

PRAYER BY: PINKIE FARMER

Father God, thank you for the freedom and safety of this country we live in. Thank you for our protection through the guidance you give to our leaders. Thank you for all branches of our armed forces. Thank you for the men and women who willingly serve and have dedicated their lives for our protection. Thank you for the families who support them as they make this sacrifice. Father, thank you for giving soldiers the mindset and strength to succeed in those things that need to be done from day to day. They have this because you, O God, are the Great Commander-in-Chief, and we acknowledge you as you direct their paths.

Guide the Air Force as it soars through the heavens looking for unidentified planes that might cause harm to our country. As they place their feet on the first step of their aircraft, guide them with your hand. Bless their pilots with eagles' eyes as they search for threats high and low. Protect them as they fly to perform the task destined for them. We pray for them to receive your help in this endeavor.

Guide the Army and the Marines as they trample through unsafe areas in foreign lands at the command of their leaders. Bless their feet to move away from harm as you walk before them. When they gain territory, we thank you for the victory.
Guide the Navy and the Coast Guard as they tirelessly sail the Seven Seas and our coasts, above and below. They're not always visible, but they keep us safe from threats in the water. Guide them as they travel—to and fro—across the waters to secure us. May

your eyes and hands continue to lead and instruct them in all they're required to do.

O God, these men and women of our military forces are very brave, courageous, and fearless. I pray that your presence, your power, and your anointing rests upon them in their service to you and this country. Some have the legacy of sacrificing it all. Please remember their loved ones and fulfill all their needs. Guide the government in attending to their needs and assisting them. As we honor them, may your love continue to shield and protect them in Jesus' name. Amen.

# Marriage

PRAYER BY: KEEVA DEDEWO

Lord, thank you for the sacred union of marriage and for every marriage that you have brought together. By giving us marriage, you gave us a good thing. Your word says that a man will leave his father and mother and be united with his wife to become one flesh. Your word says that no one is to separate what God has joined together. Marriage, as you created it to be, is a wonderful, joyous, and blessed union with You as its foundation. Guide husbands and wives so that they would be unified and allow you to be the center of their lives. Send your angels of protection to surround every married couple, and shelter them from the spiritual forces of evil that seek to destroy them. Preserve marriages and guide husbands and wives, so that they would be Godly examples of marriage for future generations to learn from.

Lord, now more than ever, we need you to take hold of our marriages. I pray that unwed men and women would wait on you. I pray that they would allow you to lead them to Godly marriage, and not try to do Your work for you. I pray that they would honor the vows of love, commitment, and fidelity that they bring before you. I pray that they would turn to you during tough times, not to thoughts of separation or divorce. I pray for those who bring past brokenness, unresolved hurt, and pain into their marriages - that they would turn to you as the only One who can heal, comfort, and restore. Show husbands how to love their wives as Christ loved the church and gave Himself for it. Show wives how to submit to their husbands – not by the world's understanding of submission, but by your intention. Lord, where there is a lack of understanding of your way, provide clarity. Guide husbands and wives to pray for one another. Guide them in praying together so that their unions will be strengthened and your love will prevail. Amen.

Scriptural references: Genesis 2:24; Mark 10:9; Ephesians 5:25

# Widows

PRAYER BY: ZANDER ALLEN

Father God, I come before you asking you to heal the hearts of widows who lost their loved ones and give them strength to move on in life. If we ask in your name, I know that you'll send us God-fearing companions. I thank you because I know that you will, hallelujah. We know we can't rush you because your will is your will. However long it takes, we'll be ready with open arms. Hallelujah, Father, help us be ready, willing, and able for what you're sending our way, praise the LORD. We thank you for everything you've done for us, everything you're doing, and everything you will do in Jesus' name.

Father God, we know you won't leave us and you're standing by our side. Yes, it does seem hard at times but we keep praying and believing on your word because your word doesn't change, praise your mighty name. Father, I'm asking you to heal our broken hearts. We know that you have change coming in our lives that will show everyone that our God is real and there's nobody like you, hallelujah, we praise your name. Father, we were walking through a dark tunnel but praise God, you brought us into your marvelous light. I thank you for all these things I ask of you in Jesus' mighty name. Amen. Amen. Amen.

Scriptural reference: 1 Peter 2:9

# Depression
PRAYER BY: WANDA WRIGHT

Dear God, I stand still in my spirit, asking you to help minds troubled with depression. Let them feel the warmth of your love. Send an angel of hope to take away all doubt and fear. Help them move forward into a new journey. I pray for their minds to be free. I pray for your loving Spirit to wash away their troubles. God, I pray that you give them strength and help. God, I trust only you, for you are the Alpha and Omega, the King of kings. I pray that you take their hand and lead them to better days. Amen.

# Procrastination

PRAYER BY: JESSICA FRANCOIS JOHNSON

Praise God! Hallelujah! Thank you, Jesus! Father God in the name of Jesus, you tell us in your word that everyone who worships you shall worship you in spirit and truth. O God, I ask you to help all those who procrastinate. You tell us in your word that if a man doesn't work, he won't eat. We can't go to our jobs being late and keep our jobs because you said everything is to be done in decency and in order. We know it's a spirit that's not of you because you tell us in your word that we can do all things through Christ who strengthens us. We have no reason to prolong anything that you give us the vision, the dream, and the opportunity to do.

O God, I cast out every spirit of procrastination and send it back to the pit of hell in the name of Jesus. LORD God, I ask you to strengthen your people in their weakness in the name of Jesus. Father God, you've given us power to speak things that are not as though they were. I ask you to send your help to people who have the desire to do things but can't move forward. Dear God, we cry out for your help. We thank you in advance of what we ask for in Jesus' name. Amen.

Scriptural reference: Ephesians 5:15-17

# Fivefold Ministry

PRAYER BY: APOSTLE DINA HUBERT

Father God in Jesus' name, we come before you praying and interceding for the five-fold ministry. Your word tells us that you gave us apostles, and prophets, and evangelists, and pastors, and teachers. Father, we ask you to anoint and continue to cover everyone you've called to the apostleship. We pray for your apostles to govern under your guidance. We pray for your prophets to speak under your direction. We pray for your evangelists to proclaim the gospel as commanded by your Word. We pray that your pastors will lead and feed the flock as instructed by you, and we pray for your teachers to be well-versed in the scriptures to be instructed by your Word.

Father, we dismantle every attack against the five-fold ministry. We cancel scandal and shame against your leaders in Jesus' name. We come against the spirit of division amongst them and we decree unity, peace and harmony among them in Jesus' name. We rebuke the spirit of competition in leadership, and we pray for the spirit of correction to make things right with them in their midst.

We pray that your power will keep your apostles, prophets, pastors, evangelists and teachers. We pray for them to honor their calling by walking worthily of it. We decree holiness among them in Jesus' name, so they'll be able to resist the temptations of the flesh. We pray that you calm the rush for many to become a part of the five-fold ministry. We pray for them to wait on their calling and not accelerate it based on their gifts or calling. We pray that church leaders wait on you before releasing, ordaining, or affirming people into offices without your heavenly green light in Jesus' name. Amen!

Scriptural reference: Ephesians 4:11

# Creativity

PRAYER BY: PASTOR RHONDA BOLDEN

O dear heavenly Father, we were on your mind from the beginning of time. Even when you spoke light into the midst and void of pure darkness, your Spirit and power burst through the darkness and created light. Thank you for our beautiful mothers who birthed us into this world to release the greatness you breathed into us. Thank you for breathing life in man and making us living souls full of unlimited, divine creativity! We are free to create as much as we desire without limit. Thank you, God, for using us to release millions of inventions into the land, with many more to come. We know, O God, that everything in this world –from a screw to a skyscraper, from a record album to a Rolls Royce— came not of ourselves, but through you. O God, you breathed divine creativity through us, and we thank you.

We pray, O God, that your divine creativity be released through the children of your Kingdom. Let there be such a gushing spring of new ideas that man has never seen or heard of. Let your power flow through those who are yielded, excited, and ready to receive insight from you to solve problems in the world today.

God, we thank you because divine creativity is a form of intimacy with you and we cherish that intimate time with you like no other. We pray strength and perseverance for those who are working on inventions but get a little discouraged. They run into problems with lack of money for patents, prototypes, attorneys, and finding people they can trust to help them to get things done and not steal their ideas! God, we thank you for divine cheerleaders assigned not to hinder them, but to help them, to encourage them, and provide them with resources, information, divine protection, direction, and connections.   Thank you, God, for the swift release of your supernatural favor for temporarily-delayed ideas that are now going forth in Jesus' name. I declare and decree now that there will be no more delay—NO MORE DELAY. Let your glory reign in them and through them in Jesus' name.

Thank you for the overflow of Kingdom financiers who are willing and very able to finance multimillion-dollar divine insights without hesitation.   O Lord, you can use us now…our minds, our mouths, and our hands to impact the nations. Speak Lord, speak Lord…use us to help others and encourage them to use their God-good gifts. In Jesus' name, let the breath of God in them not be in vain. Amen, and so it is!

# Balance
PRAYER BY: ALLISON WILLIAMS

Father, we thank you for your promise to refresh our tired bodies and restore our tired souls. God, right now we're in desperate need of stability in our lives. It's almost impossible for us not to get caught up in the "busyness" of everyday life and the overwhelming number of distractions competing for our time and attention, whether it's home, work, family, social media, or the current state of world affairs. Without you as the center of our stability, it's easy to get thrown off-course and feel unbalanced. Our human nature can cause us to take on more than we're capable of handling, and sometimes we find ourselves in way over our heads. Father, restore our equilibrium. Teach us how to set reasonable boundaries and remove those people and things in our lives that hinder our growth.

Lord, we know you're concerned with every aspect of our lives. We know that mental, physical, emotional and spiritual balance is important for a productive life, but sometimes we struggle to achieve it. Teach us how to live wisely and live well. Teach us how to be less preoccupied with getting things so we can respond to your giving. Help us discover Selah moments where we can pause, reflect, and prepare for what's next. When we feel overwhelmed, help us find the time to be still so we can gain clarity and perspective.

We realize that in order to recharge, we have to connect to our power source, so God, during those Selah moments, we'll take time to sit in your presence. We'll take time to allow our hearts to be uplifted and rejuvenated through praise and worship instead of the cacophony of noise in our daily lives. Give us a yearning for your word so we can learn and receive direction. Help us meditate on it and hide it in our hearts so during those times when we you feel unsteady, we have your word to draw from. Teach us how to pray, not only so we can speak to you, but so we can tune in and listen for your voice. Fill our cup so we can do the same for others. God in those moments of disparity between where we are and where we should be, help us to pause, connect, and find realignment with you. Selah.

Scriptural reference: Jeremiah 31:25

# Trauma

PRAYER BY: PASTOR RACHELE A. DIXIE

Heavenly Father, your people are in a season of distress and turmoil in this world. So many of your children have been affected by trauma. Trauma from war, from violence, from addictions, from neglect, and so much more. O Lord, we pray for your healing of those who battle against the emotional chaos that has infected their spirit man. We pray that you intervene in every place of distress, sadness, and anger. We come against flashbacks and nightmares that serve to bring in anxiety or fear. We are asking you, O Lord, to show us how to help those who suffer from trauma. Show us how to be more compassionate and understanding. Show us how to listen without judgment, and how to offer the love of Christ and the sincere milk of the Word to our hurting brothers and sisters.

Many are hiding the traumas of their past and feel they have no recourse for healing. Yet in this moment, O Lord, we speak release from darkness, from shame, and guilt. We expose the lies of the enemy and we look for the pathway to healing with great expectation. As we represent you, let us be a light in the darkness and bring hope to the hopeless. Let your love and care outshine any lie of worthlessness that the enemy has caused trauma victims to believe. Through us, let them know that they are loved and that there are means for them to receive healing in the midst of uncertainty. Lord, place your hand upon the nations. For everyone who has felt neglected and left behind because of unresolved trauma, we pray for them to experience your true presence and healing. Lord God, we believe that you will expose the enemy. Your people will no longer hide in the darkness, but they will reveal their struggles in the light. Let strongholds be broken as struggles are revealed. Let chains be loosed and the captives set free. We love you Lord, and we believe you for new life for everyone who is bound by trauma. Do it NOW, O God, as only you can. In Jesus' name. Amen.

# Understanding

PRAYER BY: JUANITA WALTERS

Father, I pray that every reader walks in the divine understanding of who you are. As we gain revelation and knowledge of who you are, I pray that deeper connections with you are cultivated with you, that our purposes are revealed, and that your wise counsel is revealed. I pray for our understanding that were created to worship you, and to give you praise and glory. I pray for our understanding that you are the Author and Finisher of our faith. You know the path that we will take and we can trust that your perfect will is best for our lives. I pray that we understand why obedience to your will and your way is better than sacrifice. I pray for our understanding that you created us in your image, that we are fearfully and wonderfully made, and that you love us with a love that is never failing. You are faithful and your word will not return to you void. You are a promise keep and your promises are yes and amen. We are a royal priesthood, a chosen generation that is favored and called out of darkness. You are our friend, our vindicator, our provider, our shield, our fortress, our peace, our solid rock, our banner, our Redeemer, our justifier, our miracle worker, our way-maker, our healer, and all that we need.

I pray that we understand that it's because of your grace and mercy that we are here today. I pray that we understand how great your sacrifice was to save us. You suffered, bled, and died so that we could have the keys to eternal life. The shedding of your blood was for the remission of our sins. Your death and resurrection conquered death, hell, and the grave. I pray that we understand why you gave us the authority to trample on snakes and scorpions, and to overcome all the power of the enemy so that nothing will harm us. I pray that we understand how no weapon formed against us shall prosper, and that we are more than conquerors through you. In our weakness, your strength is made perfect. I pray for our understanding that you shall never leave us nor forsake us. I pray for our understanding that we have a high priest which cannot be touched with the feeling of our infirmities; but was in all points tempted like as we are, yet without sin. With every temptation, He provides a way of escape. I pray for our understanding that our Lord understands rejection because He was the stone the builders rejected and who has become the cornerstone. I pray for our understanding that our God loves us beyond what the world sees. Greater is He that is in us, than he that is in the world. You will complete the great work that you began in us! I pray for our understanding that we were chosen and called by God to be the light!

Scriptural references: Proverbs 3:5-6, 14:29, 2:11-16, 18:2, 2:2-5, 4:7; Ephesians 2:8-10; 2 Timothy 2:7; Matthew 6:33; 2 Corinthians 10:3; Isaiah 55:9; James 1:2-4; Ecclesiastes 3:1-22; Colossians 4:6; 1 Corinthians 2:12; Ephesians 1:18

# Future

PRAYER BY: LINDA M. JOHNSON

Jesus, as we move forward in this life, I am so glad that you have given us an optimistic future that is full of hope, joy, love, and all goodness.

Lord, you are so precious, beautiful, and sweeter than honey that drips from the honeycomb.

Father, you know the plans you have for our lives, to give us a future full of hope, grace, mercy, prosperity, and overwhelming joy.

Dear God, in Jesus name, as your servants, we receive all that you promised us.

Let the power of your Holy Spirit lead us and guide us into all truth.

Let the fire and passion in us inspire others to improve themselves and make an impact on others they encounter.

# Lust

PRAYER BY: DAWN HILL

Dear God, I'm standing in the gap for your people, asking you to deliver us all from lust. There are so many of us who struggle with the flesh. With just a touch, a glance, or even a conversation, we can be led to cheating. If we submit ourselves to you, we'd know that sex outside of marriage is fornication. Once married and bonded together in your name, we wouldn't crave anybody but you and our spouse. Dear God, you know that our spirits are willing, but our flesh is weak. Help us keep our bodies and minds under subjection so we won't have so many heartaches, sleepless nights, or tearful days. O God, help us fill our voids with your presence, your word, your Spirit, with thoughts of your blessings, and the love you give us for staying on the path you set for us.

Give us the strength to fight off everyone and everything that tries to come between us and our spouses. Help us block out those whispering voices persuading us to cheat, hurting not only our partners, but hurting you as our God. Father, deliver us from that lusting spirit because it's not of you. We want to walk in your light and be pleasing to you. We want an everlasting love with you and with the spouses we love and care about. This lusting spirit is strong, but God, you're Almighty and nothing is impossible for you to do. We know you're able to remove temptation, O God. Help us find things to do to keep our minds from wandering. O God, I'm asking you to pour out your Spirit and help us because we can't fix this ourselves. Father, we need you. Amen.

Scriptural reference: 1 Corinthians 9:27

# Suffering

PRAYER BY: DESRENE OGILVIE

Heavenly Father, most precious Lord our Savior and King, Creator of every living thing, we thank you for being our perfect example. You were the epitome of suffering and death in this human flesh to atone all our sins on the cross at Calvary. Jesus, when you endured all physical pain, mental anguish and torment as the innocent sacrificial Lamb, you had us in mind as you took on the sins of the world. God, your Word says you were wounded because we continually transgress against you. You were bruised for our iniquities. Your inner peace was chastened in exchange for our peace of mind. Daddy God, we may feel pain and discomfort in our mental and physical state because of sudden and unexpected sickness and trauma. We may have disorders and ailments that manifested from our involvement with cares of this life, but we know we have an advocate in you. We can always place our lives in your hands.

God, we your people can have a hope that makes us not ashamed, knowing that our troubles are temporary and will not last. Through situations that we might have to suffer through and endure, we can focus on the finish line and the prize. We don't have to wait until the battle is over, we can shout now! We shout knowing that the battle has already been won and it's all working together for our good. God, we know there will be glory after this, and we have the victory over the enemy. Daddy God, you deserve all the honor, glory, and praise due to your name because you'll bring us through and make us bigger, stronger, and better than we were before. We stand on your promises. We make declare it in the earth realm, and we call it done in Jesus' name. Amen, and amen.

Scriptural reference: Romans 8:18

# POTUS

PRAYER BY: KENDRA RENEE' MANIGAULT

Heavenly Father, I pray for the president of the United States. I come before you praying that your Spirit rests upon them. I pray that skillful men and women of God would be able to minister to POTUS with wisdom and godly, knowledgeable counsel. I pray that POTUS would have ears to hear and a heart to understand what you have to say.

Father, I pray that our country will be led with more compassion, honesty, integrity, godliness, and with a more peaceable spirit. We pray against the force of wickedness in high places. You, God, are our refuge and stronghold in times of trouble. Let your wisdom speak in the White House and rule as we pray for normalcy, safety, and total healing in the land.

I pray that POTUS won't come up against the good news of the gospel of Jesus Christ, prayer, and our houses of worship. I pray that your word convicts them and saves their soul. The word of the Lord prevails, and I pray that it grows mightily and heavily upon their heart. Their knees will bow and their tongues will confess that Jesus Christ is Lord. They shall call on the name of Jesus and be saved! Amen!

Scriptural references: Romans 13:1-2; 1 Peter 2:13; Ephesians 6:12; Psalm 46:1

# Rejection

PRAYER BY: CELESTINE CISSE

Heavenly Father in the name of our Lord Jesus Christ, we believe that you are the Son of God who takes away the sins of all those who repent and confess you as Lord. We know that the blood of Jesus Christ cleanses all sins. Thank you, Lord, for making provision for deliverance from the spirit of rejection and all forms of bondage. Lord, send your axe of fire to the foundation and root of rejection. Destroy every evil plantation in the name of Jesus. Flush out every inherited satanic deposit. You are the same Son of God who spoke healing words to the woman with the spirit of infirmity, and we call on you today. You're the same Son of God who makes captives free to be free indeed. The spirit of rejection can no longer live. It is destroyed and nullified. Every imagination of low self-esteem, resentment, bitterness, indignation, wrath, bad temper, contention, slander, abuse, evil speaking, rage, insecurity, malice and spite will no longer operate. Satan, your power of evil influence is broken in the name of Jesus. Lord, we know that your word concerning healing will not return to you void, but it will accomplish what you say it will.

Now Father, release your love, compassion, understanding, grace and mercy as readily and freely as you will. It is written in your word that the love of God has been shed abroad into our hearts by the Holy Ghost whom you have given us. Father, please fill those vacant places with your redemption, your word, your Spirit, your righteousness, your revelation and your knowledge. Father, I thank you for your redeeming love by Jesus

Christ. Thank you for your promise that if we ask, we shall receive in Jesus' name. Amen.

Scriptural references: Luke 13:10-13; John 8:36

# Bitterness

PRAYER BY: SHARON FRANK

God of peace, help us to be more like you each day. We pray against our flesh right now and declare that we put away bitterness, wrath, and anger, for these are not your attributes. They come from a place of darkness. Life can be extremely disheartening sometimes and it causes us to feel bitter within. Even Job could not restrain his mouth and complained in the bitterness of his soul, but you did not call us to be a bitter people. Even when we face persecution in the world, your Son commands us to be of good cheer because He conquered the world. In you, we have our peace and we embrace this word over our lives today. Today, we welcome peace in our hearts with open arms so that it surpasses all understanding and guards our hearts and minds in Christ Jesus. We receive peace, not as the world gives, but the divine peace that you freely give in Jesus' name.

Give us peace so we may forgive all who have hurt us in the past. Lord, for those who sinned against us, teach us how to forgive them seventy times seven times like you told Peter. Father, your Word emphasizes that we should not hold bitterness in our hearts. We must store love within ourselves, so help us to always demonstrate love —even when it's difficult to do so. We pray that we do not deal with people in a bitter or unforgiving manner because if so, that is how you—the Righteous Judge—will deal with us. Fill us with more of your love so we can extend it those around us daily. Bitterness is draining, but love bears all things, believes all things, hopes all things and endures all things! Heavenly Father, we pray that you create in us pure hearts. Remove our bitter hearts and renew a steadfast spirit within us! Forgive us for the many occasions that we have chosen to be bitter. Heal us and help us so that we can be well again. Thank you, dear Lord. Amen.

Scriptural references: Ephesians 4:31; Job 10:1; John 16:33, 14:27; Philippians 4:7; 1 Corinthians 13:7

# Living Sacrifice

PRAYER BY: VIDA WILLIAMS

God, we humbly come to you for guidance and assistance in showing us how to offer ourselves as living sacrifices to you. We fall short. We stumble and fall. Our flesh interferes with our Christian discipleship. God, we want to forget ourselves and keep our minds directed by your guidance. We know you love us because we're your children. God, we thank you because you love us and show mercy for us over and over again. We no longer offer animal sacrifices. As living sacrifices, we give you our souls, our bodies, and our minds. Jesus, we fall in love with you over and over again, and the best of our lives is still ahead of us. Day by glorious day, we know we're getting closer to heaven because we feel your presence in our  hearts.

Father, sometimes we're faced with peer pressure and become afraid of our Christianity. Christianity can be a difficult and lonely road to travel. We want to become better Christians and make our lives better for you. Show  us how to love those who persecute us. We need your power to keep our bodies holy and sacred for you. We have to refrain from sexual immorality so that we can show the world the example of true Christian sacrifice. God, you're an amazing Father. You sacrificed your only Son, Jesus Christ, for us. He died on the cross so we could have abundant life. We want to serve you in committed worship and not with meaningless rituals. We must remove ourselves from this world and its satanic nature. We must keep our minds stayed on you. Every day, we need your power to turn away from this world and surrender ourselves to you. Give us the courage to do your will and separate ourselves from this world of lies.

Hold our hands with your unchanging hand. With our faith, help us follow your voice inside and live truthful and fulfilling lives. Protect us from danger seen and unseen. Because of your love, show us how to be better Christians by loving and forgiving others. We thank you for your strong voice within telling us to be still and not follow the crowd. Through silence and solitude, we can be more like you. With patience, we wait on you and study your Word to become better Christians. Lord, keep us near. Thank you for loving us and showing us undeserved mercy. Amen.

# Supernatural Favor

PRAYER BY: APOSTLE LYDIA WOODSON-SLOLEY

LORD, we thank you for the supernatural power of your favor. You extend it, even when we don't deserve it. Help us recognize your divine intervention in our personal affairs as your favor extends toward us when we least expect it. LORD, we thank you for your thoughts being higher than ours, and for your ways being higher than ours. With your all-seeing ability, you're able to impart supernatural favor before we realize that we need it. LORD, you shield us, you protect us, you supply all our needs, you show up in our time of trouble, you heal our bodies, and you comfort our souls with a touch of favor over our lives. For all this, we thank you and we love you in JESUS' matchless name. Amen.

Scriptural reference: Psalm 5:12

# Depression

PRAYER BY: NINA D. BROWN

O Lord, how do we make it stop? This indescribable pain, a pain that has left us disconnected and heartbroken as we watch the reruns of our despair become a permanent reminder of our suffering. The constant infighting of this affliction becomes our blanket of protection from cold stares and silent whispers. Between resentment and rejection, they argue within our souls: who will be first today?

The despair of each moment has become the foundation that cover the scars inflicted by our hands, but we are unable to escape the source of the torture we caused. Each tear is transformed into comical interludes with punchlines of undiscernible chants of our failures and heartbreaks. So how do you justify the suffering connected to this untraceable source which now highlights our very existence?

Lord, we wish to surrender, take rest, but no course of action grants us access to this request. Where is this peace connected to the paradise that speaks of the joy and love connected to the mention of your name? Send us proof of eternal paradise in this place.

Lord, O Lord, provide a preview of past battles won. Reveal secrets connected to the manifestation of lies associated with unfulfilled promises masked by the false presentation of our now reality. Our souls cry because they thirst after you. Our flesh is winning but our spirits are determined not to quit –yet, we grow weary. Help us, Lord, help us navigate and outsmart the false representation of our now reality.

Please help us exhale pain and misery, and help us inhale life, joy, love, and peace. Help us exhale isolation and sorrow, inhale grace and mercy, exhale lies and discouragement, and inhale your strength and power to withstand what rises against you, Grant us the fortitude to stand and see the salvation of the Lord. Protect our minds as we fight this war that desires to overtake us. Lord, breathe on us as you guide us out of this place of pain into your arms of safety, for in you shall we receive rest and restoration.

Scriptural reference: Psalms 69:1-3

# Healing

PRAYER BY: BILLIE OGLESBY

Father in the name of Jesus, we come boldly to your throne thanking you for what you've done and what you're continuously doing. Before the foundation of the world, you put provisions in place for us to speak and declare healing against everything that works against us physically and emotionally. From the beginning to the end, it's your perfect will for us to be whole – inside and out.

Heavenly Father, when we pray, we stand before you having the confidence that your healing power is released through our mouths and manifested in our bodies. The price was already paid at Calvary as part of your redemptive plan for us. It's our prayer that your healing power is manifested in our bodies to negate lies, fear, and doubt. You remind us throughout your word that we have an inheritance that rightfully belong to us. We declare and decree that we'll operate in faith. We'll hold fast to your unchanging word and be thankful until healing comes. Lord, in Jesus' name, we focus and apply your word to every physical symptom that we face.

Father, healing is your unchangeable will for us. It's not automatic, but we ask and receive it by faith just as we received our new birth by faith. We thank you Father, for healing is our right as born-again children of God. Throughout your word, you remind us of our inheritance and admonish us to live in the fullness of our rights. Healing is not an unreachable part of the gospel. Lord, you commissioned the sick to be healed when you came to preach the good news, so we acknowledge healthy bodies in Jesus' name. Your word says you sent your word; you healed them and delivered them from their destruction. God, you always provided healing for your creation. While you were here on earth, you continually spoke deliverance and healing, and that hasn't changed. You're still our healer. Lord, we appreciate the wonderful gift of healing and the power of your blood to sustain us. Lord Jesus, we thank you for the performance of your word. Amen, and amen.

Scriptural reference: Psalm 107:20

# Guidance

PRAYER BY: PATRICIA ETHEAH

O Lord, help us to follow you. Let not our will, but your will be done. Lord, O Lord, we need your guidance. We need your help because we cannot see our way clear enough to go forward in the things we desire. Lord, help us to wait, to watch, and to continue praying and praising you for those things. We will know because your Spirit and word will be confirmed and confirmation will follow. Lord, thank you for allowing us to trust your guidance. Please guide us in the way we should go. Thank you for your unconditional love. Thank you for hearing our request. Lord, help us to obey your will for the rest of our lives and for our will to submit to yours. If we look up to the hills from where cometh our help, we know you will help us. Help us to stay humble and to not stand in our own understanding. We pray for discernment to see before we react in Jesus' name. Make our crooked places straight. Show us how to wait on your timing and be still in our waiting. Please guide us with your eyes so we can move forward with the direction of your Holy Spirit.

Lord, you said no one is perfect but you! therefore we trust in your word. We walk and we hold on to you so we can reach our destiny. Lord, help us in our spirit and help us not to lean on our own thinking. Help us focus on your word and walk it out in our lives. Your word has strength and power when we are weak and hopeless. We need to remember your promises for our lives. It's about waiting and timing, and not going ahead of you. Without you, we can go nowhere far. Lord, help us to seek your Kingdom first so that you can direct us in the way we should go. We know that when we wait and meditate on your word, we can do as you would do. When we believe that we can do it all on our own, we fail and mess up all that you entrusted us to do, amen. Help screams out from our spirit because we know there is no good in us. Lord, our prayer and our cry is to be humble and allow you to guide us into your truth. Amen, and amen.

Scriptural references: Jeremiah 10:23; Proverbs 14:12; Psalm 119:12, 25:4, 48:14; John 10:27; Matthew 6:33

# Parents

PRAYER BY: GLORIA FONDJO

As we grow up within our families, we're made and shaped by those who raise us. Their actions and decisions ultimately affect who we end up becoming to the world and to the next generation. Lord, we pray that you enlighten parents to make wise decisions for their kids. As guides, please give parents the strength, courage and wisdom they need to raise faithful servants in your Kingdom. Lord, may they be inspired to act on your behalf and do as you would do, and not as society makes them believe they should. Inspire them to teach their kids to love themselves first. Inspire them to teach their kids to love each other as they love themselves, to appreciate their peers, to be kind, grateful, compassionate, and to always keep in mind that they live to serve the Kingdom of the Lord. Help them remember that things are made to be used, and people were made to be loved, and not the other way around.

Dear Father, help our parents recognize the big role they play in our lives. Give them humility to recognize and apologize when they do wrong. At the end of the day, parenting is a learning journey, not a skill. Help new parents gracefully find their way to you so that you may guide them as they go. Father, help them guide new life to you and teach their children how to differentiate their will from your will. Lord we thank you for showing up in our lives through our parents. May you always keep them safe. May they always be proud of their legacy. Father, let all generational curses be broken in your sacred name. May you replace them with generational blessings that honor your almighty name. In Jesus' name, amen.

Scriptural reference: Ephesians 6:4

# Grief

PRAYER BY: ANTIONETTE LESLIE-HOLLAND

Dear Father God in heaven, thank you for all your mercy and goodness. I thank you for your love and guidance every day. Heavenly Father, you have fearfully and wonderfully made us. You knew us before we came into this world and you know the ending of our lives. Lord hear me as I pray. I pray for those who are mourning and grieving over the loss of loved ones. Comfort their broken hearts in grieving over loved ones lost in the present and in the past. Strengthen those who feel they cannot move on.

We are guided by your divine Word that tells us joy will come in the morning. We know that these aren't just mere words, but holy words coming from you. You let us know that the joy of the Lord is our strength. You give us the strength to cope with losing loved ones. When we remember them, let us not remember them with tears of sadness, but with tears of joy and happiness for knowing that our loved ones are no longer in pain and suffering. Lord, may we continue to read your word to build our faith in you and to encourage others.  We know death is part of life, so I pray that our loved ones knew Jesus Christ as their Lord and Savior. In the name of Father, the Son, and the precious Holy Ghost, I pray. Amen.

Scriptural references: Psalm 30:5, 29:11

# Unemployment

PRAYER BY: MINISTER TYRA FRAZIER

O God, how excellent and majestic is your name. How sovereign is your name. Lord, we worship and adore you. We come to you with humbled hearts and gratitude. We come into your presence with love and thanksgiving for all that you have done, O God. Before we send up our petitions, we want to tell you we love and adore you, O God. We honor your presence and we speak well of you on today. We thank you for your kindness and faithfulness. We thank you for always being God in our lives. We thank you for being our way-maker and provider. We call you Jehovah-Jireh, our provider. We call you Jehovah Shalom, our peace. We call you El Shaddai, our Lord God Almighty, and we call you El Elohim, the everlasting God. We call you holy and righteous name because you are things to all people. Now Lord, we pray for those who are in need of a blessing. We come on behalf of your people who stand in need of job. We come now asking for favor for those who are submitting applications online and in person. We come now for those who are searching desperately for the means to provide for their families.

God, we know that you are a provider so we ask for your hand of mercy every time they hit the send button. We pray for your hand of mercy every time they complete a job application. We pray for your hand of mercy every time they interview for a position. We pray for clarity of speech, sincerity, and honesty in the name of Jesus. We pray for favor with man and any person who will interview your people. God, we pray that you open doors for those who are actively seeking jobs. Send unexpected income to those who stand in financial need. Sustain them until they can obtain gainful employment. Allow them to find favor with their debt collectors and eliminate some of their debt. Wipe the slate clean, O God. Give them a fresh start and let their credit not be affected in this season from the loss of employment. God, I know you can do it because your word tells us to ask what we will in your name and it shall be done. God, we come asking in faith, praying that you have heard the cries and pleas, and that have seen the tears of your people. Be God in their lives and come through one more time. In the name of Jesus, I pray. Amen.

# Men

PRAYER BY: MOZELLEN DOBIE

Heavenly Father, I come in the matchless name of Jesus. Creator of all things, God, you are the very air that we breathe. Lord, I pray on behalf of men. You spoke the word and made man in your image. You breathed into his nostrils and he became a living soul, thank you Jesus. You said what you made was good because you're a good God, thank you Jesus. God, I pray for the strength of man. I pray for the peace of man. I pray for the mind of man. We're living in perilous times. Men are becoming lovers of themselves more than lovers of God. I pray that their hearts turn to you and they seek your face, thank you Jesus. I pray for them to cover their wives and be protectors of their families. God, you created man to serve you. You have a plan for the life of your creation; a plan for good and not for evil, thank you Jesus.

Heavenly Father, you gave man dominion over everything. I pray that men take their rightful place. I pray they receive you as their Lord and Savior and be filled with the Holy Ghost. Jesus, I pray that men realize they are a royal priesthood. Hallelujah, thank you, Jesus! The devil comes to rob, steal, kill and destroy, but you came to give life. I pray that men live their lives to please you and lift up the name of Jesus. Lord, please protect young men and keep them focused. Help them come to know you at an early age. Hallelujah! Help older men teach younger men. Jesus, I pray that wives lift up their husbands in prayer as they stand by them being good helpmates. God, you made man the head and not the tail, the lender and not the borrower to above and not beneath, hallelujah, thank you, Jesus. God, I pray that men everywhere realize how they need the word of God to order their steps. I pray for men to study your word. Your word leads, teaches, and guides to all truth. Your word is life. God, your word is strength, hallelujah, thank you Jesus. As I lift up all men to you, I pray that your love, peace, and protection covers them in Jesus' name.

Scriptural reference: Romans 12:1

# Agriculture

PRAYER BY: VERNETTA DRUMMOND-MERCER

Father God in the name of Jesus, we thank you and we give you glory for all things. We thank you for your many benefits that you give us daily. Lord, you said you would bless those who put their trust in you. You said you would make us to be like trees growing vibrantly. We won't have to be afraid when seasons change because our leaves will remain green. When there is no rain, we won't worry because we will continue to bear fruit. God, you said you would open up the heavens, the storehouse of your bounty, to send rain upon the land in the right season and you would bless the work of our hands. You said we would lend to many nations and borrow from none.

We thank you for the agriculture of our nation that is a major part of our survival and a foundation to our economic system. Lord, give us dew to enrich the earth with abundance of grain. We thank you for overflow in the supernatural and for the manifestation in the natural. Lord, help us pay careful attention to herds and to know, through prayer and seeking your face, the condition of your flocks. Father, allow the earth to bring forth vegetation and yield good seed. You said in your word that if one planted and another one watered, that you would give the increase. As we pray, we pray with the intention of believing, that through mustard seed faith, anything is possible through you. We thank you because we know that you are able. You can do anything but fail.

As we repent, we ask you to renew the soil in which we grow our food. Preserve the earth from the wickedness of men and forgive us for our misuse and mistreatment of it!   Help us cultivate our plants and care for livestock in order to have food supply to sustain human civilization. Lord, we thank you for allowing agriculture to shift our nation by providing us with wealth. Please bless our food processors to clear contamination from our foods. We thank you for giving humanity the wisdom to create these systems. Amen.

Scriptural reference: Psalm 24:1

# Incarceration

PRAYER BY: DR. LESLIE DUROSEAU

Vindicate me, O God, and defend my cause. O God for how long, O God, where is our help?   Daily do we seek your face, for our help comes from the Lord. How long must we live like caged animals without a master? for you are our Lord, our Master, and our King. Free us from those things that keep us bound.

El Shaddai, the Almighty God, our bodies are shackled but our minds are free in you.   Release us dear Lord from those things that restrain us. Free us from those things that keep us from the truth of who we are in you and the truth of who you are in all of us. Bless those who watch over us and care for us. They are your messengers, your servants who come to feed us our daily bread and bring us manna from heaven.

We need you Lord, for our help comes from you alone, the great God. Forgive us and do not despise us forever. Extend your mercy and your grace to us, for we are still your beloved children. Some have strayed from you, and others are innocent victims.

We turn from our wicked ways. We humble ourselves and seek your face. We are cast down but not broken, for our hope, our trust, and all that we are is placed in your capable hands.

We are humbled as we cry out Abba, Father, hear our prayers. Your ear is close to the brokenhearted, to those who are in trouble. You, God, are our way of escape. Free us, O Lord, for you are the God of justice, peace and righteousness. Amen.

Scriptural reference: Habakkuk 1:2-5

# About The Author
BIO: TENARIA DRUMMOND-SMITH

Tenaria Drummond-Smith, an ambitious and multi-talented entrepreneur, is the founder and visionary of Awesome Women On The Move, Inc., a personal ministry birthed in 2006 that has blossomed into a movement and an organization that promotes fellowship and unity among all women with the love of God through Jesus Christ. A native New Yorker and former civil service employee, a series of life changes motivated her to reinvent herself. She is totally souled-out as a servant of the gospel and will gladly spend her time ministering to anyone who wants to know about His grace and mercy toward her. She is a living testimony of what the power of God has done in her life and will freely tell others how He can change their lives for the better.

Tenaria has a strong passion for bringing women together from all walks of life and she emphasizes the display of love to everyone she meets. Experienced as a craft maker and event organizer, she loves giving back to the community. The breakthrough publishing of Tenaria's first book, *I've Been Hurt In The Church*, jumpstarted her growing list of personal and professional achievements, including becoming a bestselling author. Awesome Women On The Move has an established Facebook.com presence of 920,000+ followers (in conjunction with the Awesome Women On The Move Blog, also on Facebook), while Tenaria has a growing social media presence as a one-woman industry through Instagram, LinkedIn, and YouTube. Tenaria has the God-given vision and heart to celebrate women who do phenomenal things but are rarely recognized, and her purpose is serve as a platform to showcase women who have impacted the lives of others around them. Following her first release were two additional books co-authored with women who were willing to tell their stories of pain, inspiration, and encouragement (*Awesome Women On The Move* and *Love Grounded By Grace*). This new venture has shown Tenaria that God is not done with her yet.

# Back Cover Co-Authors

(Names below coincide with back cover images from left to right)

1    Tenaria Drummond-Smith (Author)
2    Sophia L. Greene
3    Roberta Jones-Johnson
4    Prophetess Von Brand
5    Annetta Drummond
6    Queen Mother
7    Janet Lennox
8    Dawn Grantham
9    Miranda Rivers
10   Sarah Nichols
11   Cameo Boone
12   Cyrinthia Hill-Flowers
13   Joyce Rollins
14   Cheryln Oliver-McKay
15   Esther Burgess
16   Theresa Byrd
17   Pastor Shawn Quallo

| | |
|---|---|
| 18 | Jacquelene Scruggs |
| 19 | Wendyann Williams |
| 20 | Sherrell D. Mims |
| 21 | D.D. Houston Dupree |
| 22 | Jean Thompson |
| 23 | Lesley George |
| 24 | Pinkie Farmer |
| 25 | Keeva Dedewo |
| 26 | Zander Allen |
| 27 | Wanda Wright |
| 28 | Jessica Francois Johnson |
| 29 | Apostle Dina Hubert |
| 30 | Pastor Rhonda Bolden |
| 31 | Allison Williams |
| 32 | Pastor Rachele A. Dixie |
| 33 | Juanita Walters |
| 34 | Linda M. Johnson |
| 35 | Dawn Hill |
| 36 | Desrene Ogilvie |
| 37 | Kendra Renee' Manigault |
| 38 | Celestine Cisse |
| 39 | Sharon Frank |
| 40 | Vida Williams |
| 41 | Apostle Lydia Woodson-Sloley |
| 42 | Nina D. Brown |
| 43 | Kandra Albury |
| 44 | Billie Oglesby |
| 45 | Patricia Etheah |
| 46 | Gloria Fondjo |
| 47 | Apostle Martha Green |
| 48 | Antionette Leslie-Holland |
| 49 | Minister Tyra Frazier |
| 50 | Mozellen Dobie |
| 51 | Vernetta Drummond-Mercer |
| 52 | Dr. Leslie Duroseau |

AWESOME WOMEN ON THE MOVE

# NATIONAL PRAYER BOOK

PRAYING FOR

*Everything under the Sun*

CPSIA information can be obtained
at www.ICGtesting.com
Printed in the USA
LVHW022247310720
662083LV00005B/206